CU00919195

How to Train Your
American Pit Bull Terrier

liz palika

Photo by Isabelle Francais

AMERICAN PIT BULL TERRIER

Photos by the author unless otherwise credited.

The publisher would like to thank all of the owners of dogs pictured in this book, including the following: Chris Adelman, JoEllen Adelman, Waskar Cruz, Orrin "Lee" Fitzgerald, Susan Hickey, Petra Horn, Beth Jones, Fernando Lajara, Joey Lopez, Eugene Mikell, Joe Rice, David Wilson

© T.F.H. Publications, Inc.

Distributed in the UNITED STATES to the Pet Trade by T.F.H. Publications, Inc., 1 TFH Plaza, Neptune City, NJ 07753; on the Internet at www.tfh.com; in CANADA by Rolf C. Hagen Inc., 3225 Sartelon St., Montreal, Quebec H4R 1E8; Pet Trade by H & L Pet Supplies Inc., 27 Kingston Crescent, Kitchener, Ontario N2B 2T6; in ENGLAND by T.F.H. Publications, PO Box 74, Havant PO9 5TT; in AUSTRALIA AND THE SOUTH PACIFIC by T.F.H. (Australia), Pty. Ltd., Box 149, Brookvale 2100 N.S.W., Australia; in NEW ZEALAND by Brooklands Aquarium Ltd., 5 McGiven Drive, New Plymouth, RD1 New Zealand; in SOUTH AFRICA by Rolf C. Hagen S.A. (PTY.) LTD., P.O. Box 201199, Durban North 4016, South Africa; in JAPAN by T.F.H. Publications, Japan—Jiro Tsuda, 10-12-3 Ohjidai, Sakura, Chiba 285, Japan. Published by T.F.H. Publications, Inc.

MANUFACTURED IN THE
UNITED STATES OF AMERICA
BY T.F.H. PUBLICATIONS, INC.

contents

INTRODUCTION

Most people who love animals know that many species are facing extinction. Habitat destruction, encroaching human residences, pollution, and many other factors obliterate entire species. Once a species is gone, it's gone.

We are used to hearing about wild species that we are trying to save. Humans have gone to extraordinary lengths to try and preserve some species, such as the North American black-footed ferret. But how far will we go to try and save a breed of dog?

The American Pit Bull Terrier may well be a vanishing breed. Today, this loyal, courageous breed is facing a hostile media, an unforgiving court system, and potentially, its own death knell.

Today's Pit Bulls have a long history—going back to the ancient Greeks and Romans—as fighting dogs working with and protecting mankind. Unfortunately, those fighting traits have made the breed a favorite among people who encourage aggression in their dogs. This encouragement, along with a lack of good training, poor socialization, and ignorant breeding practices have caused numerous disasters with Pit Bulls as central players.

When a dog—any dog—kills a child, mauls a senior citizen, or attacks nonthreatening neighbors, the account will make headlines. If the breed is one that has already had some bad press, such as Pit Bulls, the media goes wild. Recently, a Pit Bull Terrier mauled and killed a small child in Southern California. After the media account of the incident, hundreds of Pit Bulls were turned into local animal shelters by their worried owners. Because of the tremendous influx of dogs that had been (for the most part) poorly trained (if at all) and probably poorly socialized, animal control officials said that most of the dogs would not be considered adoptable and most would be euthanized.

Unfortunately, incidents like this are happening more and more often, not just in Southern California, but in places all over the country. Many locales have passed breed-specific legislation banning Pit Bull Terrier ownership, and some insurance companies will not insure homeowners with Pit Bulls. Some dog trainers will not allow Pit Bulls to attend group dog training classes, and many doggie day care centers will not allow Pit Bulls to be a part of the groups.

If these trends continue, it will be more and more difficult to own a Pit Bull Terrier, and the breed will face almost certain extinction. However, it doesn't have to be that way. My sister and brother-in-law have a wonderful Pit Bull that is gentle, well trained, and very much a part of the family. He is well socialized and plays well with their children and with other dogs. He is even a certified therapy dog that visits at local nursing homes and residential care facilities. Dillon pulls a wagon, too, and will give the family and neighborhood kids rides.

Interestingly, Dillon is not unusual. There are many wonderful, loyal, well-trained, and well-socialized Pit Bulls living quiet lives all over the country. We only hear about the horrible dogs; we don't hear about the good dogs with responsible owners. However, if Pit Bull enthusiasts want to see their favorite breed survive, they need to be more outspoken about its good qualities. Let's show people that Pit Bulls do make good family dogs, that they can be trained well, and that they can be loyal, protective, courageous family pets. People need to see that Pit Bulls can serve as therapy dogs, giving love to everyone they visit, and that Pit Bulls can participate ably in dog sports. The breed's survival may very well depend on this type of visibility.

Despite their reputation as aggressive dogs, well-trained Pit Bulls make excellent family pets. They are loyal, loving, and good with children.

american pit bull terrier

SELECTING
the Right Dog for You

WHAT ARE AMERICAN PIT BULL TERRIERS?

In the Beginning

American Pit Bull Terriers share an ancestry with many of the bull and mastiff-type breeds of dog. The ancient Greeks and Romans valued the big, strong mastiff-type warrior dogs that could fight alongside men in battle. The Romans also used fighting dogs in their entertainments, pitting the dogs against wild and domestic animals or armed men. When the Romans invaded Britain, they were impressed by the British war dogs, and many of these were sent back home to be bred and crossed with their fighting dogs.

Historical artworks and tapestries throughout European history show dogs of the mastiff and bull dog types. In 395 AD, the Roman historian Symmachus wrote about Bulldogs from Britain that fought gamely against armed men in the Roman circuses. Spanish tapestries of the 16th and 17th centuries depict Spanish dogs taking part in stag

The imposing Pit Bull was a warrior dog in ancient times, loyal and affectionate toward his master but ruthless toward his master's enemy.

Photo by Isabelle Francais

american pit bull terrier

and boar hunts. These dogs are broad-chested, strong-shouldered, and wide-mouthed. Similar dogs are portrayed in Roman, British, German, and Spanish art, which shows that these dogs were favored in many different societies of those eras.

In Britain, the Bulldog was created by breeding Mastiffs to create a smaller, more agile dog that was used to fight bulls and bears. Jacqueline O'Neil, a Pit Bull enthusiast and author of *The American Pit Bull Terrier*, said that the blood sports, which included dogfighting as well as bull and bear fights, were popular entertainment in England, not just for working people, but also for the royal families. The Bulldog used for many of these fights looked little like today's Bulldog; this dog had longer legs, straighter front legs, and a longer muzzle.

Experts differ as to when (and which) terriers were added to the Bulldog strains. Some historians believe that English Terriers, Fox Terriers, or Black and Tan Terriers were crossed with Bulldogs to create a dog that was courageous, tenacious, and game (like the Bulldog), but with the spirit and agility of the terrier. These dogs were called Bull and Terrier Dogs, Pit Dogs, or Pit Bullterrier dogs.

The blood sports were as popular in early America as they were in England. Although laws against blood sports were enacted as early as the 1600s, bearbaiting, bullbaiting, dogfighting, and rat-killing exhibitions were not at all uncommon; even under the threat of arrest. Most of the dogs used in these contests were either imported from England or were bred from English imports. However, as the blood sports continued in the US, Americans made their mark on the breed that would become known as the American Pit Bull Terrier.

The "Bulldog" that was used as a fighting dog in British blood sports looked more like today's Pit Bull than a modern English Bulldog.

Photo by Isabelle Francais

Photo by Isabelle Francais

As early Americans settled the frontier, they valued Pit Bulls for the breed's ability to guard the home, herd livestock, kill rodents and predators, and still serve as a loving family pet.

In early America, the breed was favored by many for its versatility. The dogs were used for many purposes: guarding the home or farm, herding livestock, chasing off predators, killing rodents, and serving as the children's companion. As Americans moved westward, their dogs went with them, including their Pit Bulls. During this time period, the American Pit Bull began to develop his unique American look. The dogs became taller than their English counterparts, more barrel-chested, and more powerful.

The United Kennel Club (UKC) was founded in 1898 with the American Pit Bull Terrier as its first recognized breed. Generations of pedigrees of fighting dogs were turned over to the UKC to establish its records. Many of today's dogs can trace their pedigrees back to some of the first registered dogs.

Pit Bulls have made a name for themselves in the US apart from their dogfighting roots. They have served as military dogs fighting human battles. Jacqueline O'Neil noted that a Pit Bull named Stubby was the most decorated canine soldier of World War I. Also, the first Pit Bull movie star was Pete, a

The Pit Bull's distinctive head is wide and flat, with a large, well-muscled jaw.

Photo by Robert Pearcy

brindle and white dog who starred in the *Little Rascals* and *Our Gang* movie shorts.

Many American celebrities, including Thomas Edison, Helen Keller, Fred Astaire, and President Theodore Roosevelt have owned Pit Bulls. More recent owners include actor Michael J. Fox.

The American Pit Bull Terrier Today

The Pit Bull today is a compact, muscular dog often referred to as the strongest dog in the world for his size. Height and weight vary according to the dog's size, but most males are between 35 and 60 pounds and females are between 30 and 50 pounds.

The Pit Bull's head is one of his most distinctive features. Often described as "brick-like," the head should be wide under the ears to allow for a wide jaw. The top of the skull is flat and there is a definite stop between the head and the muzzle. The jaw is wide and well-muscled. When the dog opens his mouth, the muscling should be apparent at the sides of the jaw. The lower jaw should not be undershot, nor should the upper lips be hanging or loose; instead, the lips should be tight. The ears can be cropped, but

today, more are left uncropped.

The neck and shoulders are well muscled and powerful, leading into a strong back and barrel-like, rounded chest. The legs are large-boned without appearing heavy. The tail is broad at the base, well anchored to the body, and carried low.

When moving, the steps should be effortless and athletic, with no wasted motion. The dog should at all times convey the impression of fitness, athleticism, and power.

Temperament

Because Pit Bulls originated as a fighting breed descended from hundred of years of fighting dogs, people assume that Pit Bulls are vicious, aggressive dogs. In reality, there is nothing further from the truth.

Historically, dogs used to hunt stag or boar or fight bears were still companion dogs to their owners. These dogs were ruthless when fighting, but they still needed to be trainable and dependable with people. For example, prior to a dogfight, the owners of opposing dogs would bathe each other's dogs. This would ensure the dog had not been coated with a drug or poison. If a dog could not be

Photo by Robert Pearcy

A high-energy Pit Bull makes a great pal for a high-energy kid.

american pit bull terrier

Photo by Isabelle Francais

Because of their long history as fighting dogs, many Pit Bulls react violently to challenges from other dogs. However, a well-trained Pit Bull can be taught to ignore them.

handled by someone else to go through this process, he was worthless as a fighting dog. In addition, getting a dog ready for the fight required hours of training and preparation. A vicious dog would not be worth the time and effort.

Today, Pit Bulls are still courageous protectors and will guard the family and their possessions. (Pity the burglar who attempts to break into the house where a Pit Bull is guarding his family.) However, when not on guard duty, the family Pit Bull is sweet-natured, happy, and a joy to spend time with. Friends are greeted with a smile (as only a Pit Bull can smile) and not just a wagging tail but an entire wagging body.

AGGRESSION TOWARD OTHER DOGS

A Pit Bull will not back down from a challenge. If, while out on a walk, another dog challenges a Pit Bull by barking, growling, or posturing, a Pit Bull will react. Generations of breeding for a fighting temperament will surface. However, a good obedience training program can serve you well. Pit Bulls can be taught to stop a challenge by looking away and ignoring the other dog's poor behavior.

DOGFIGHTING TODAY

Unfortunately, dogfighting still exists today even though it has been illegal for many years. It survives as an underground sport, and many Pit Bulls have suffered at the hands of dogfighters. Recently, police and animal control officers raided a Southern California dogfighting ring. Television crews recorded the sight of many dogs, mostly Pit Bulls, as they were loaded into the animal control vans. Most of the dogs were covered with scars and wounds, many were missing ear flaps, and some bore signs of inexpert stitching of wounds. Most of the dogs had to be euthanized.

Pit Bulls have a strong desire to please their owners and are highly trainable. They can be stubborn, however, and often have a mind of their own. But with a good training routine, this stubbornness can often be channeled in the right direction. Pit Bulls are high-energy dogs and need a lot of daily exercise. Without it, this energy can cause destructive behavior around the house and yard. Pit Bulls also enjoy being the center of attention. According to Pit Bulls, you should not be having any fun unless they are a part of it. That means the dog will want to be a part of your kid's birthday party and all holiday celebrations. This often clownlike personality makes Pit Bulls great trick training dogs and wonderful therapy dogs. Teach a Pit Bull a few tricks, give him an audience, and you'll laugh for hours.

Problem Pit Bulls

As we know from newspaper and television news headlines, there are some bad Pit Bulls. When a Pit Bull "goes bad," unfortunately, the consequences are horrible. What causes a bad dog? There are a few reasons:

A Pit Bull that is chained in the backyard all day is often depressed and angry and may develop problem behaviors.

Photo by Isabelle Francais

american pit bull terrier

• Poor breeding practices—Breeders must be aware of how genetics work and must consciously breed to produce dogs that are physically and emotionally sound. Ignorant breeding practices can produce unsafe, dangerous dogs.

• Poor socialization and training—All dogs need socialization and training as puppies to help them cope with the world around them.

• Bad training—Some people want to have an aggressive dog and train their dog to be that way. Unless you are an expert at law enforcement dog or schutzhund training, this is a dangerous type of training to pursue.

• Aggression begets aggression—Very harsh, forceful training techniques can cause a dog to resent his training and trainer. Unfair or overly hard corrections or punishments can cause a dog to fight back.

• Chaining the dog—Dogs, including Pit Bulls, that are chained in the backyard (to a stake or doghouse) are prone to develop problem behaviors. A chained dog is vulnerable to every passing stray dog and every child who wishes to tease

or torment the dog. These dogs are often bored, frustrated, morose, depressed, and angry.

IS A PIT BULL THE RIGHT DOG FOR YOU?

Evaluating Your Personality and Lifestyle

The decision to add a dog to your family is not a decision to be taken lightly. Pit Bulls live 12 to 14 years and require some special care and attention from you.

Do you work long hours and come home tired? When you come home, do you want to kick back, put up your feet, and relax? If you do, then a Pit Bull is not the right dog for you. You might be better off with a cat or with an older dog of a quieter, more sedate breed. A Pit Bull would not be able to tolerate your long hours away from home and the lack of activity with you.

Do you work away from home for long hours but like to get outside and do things when you come home? If you do, then you might want to consider adopting an adult Pit Bull rather than getting a puppy. Puppies require a lot of time with you, whereas an adult dog might be able to cope with your time away as long as you could spend time with the dog when you are at home.

When you have a Pit Bull, you are the center of that dog's world. He will want to follow you around the house, even to the bathroom. If you can't handle this type of closeness, don't get a Pit Bull; you will break his heart by pushing him away.

Before you get a Pit Bull, look at your life as realistically as possible. A Pit Bull can be a wonderful companion for some people, but he is not the right dog for everyone. A Pit Bull should not be left at home alone for too long each day; if you work 10 to 12 hours a day,

that's too much. A Pit Bull shouldn't be owned by someone who doesn't treasure a dog's closeness. Nor should a Pit Bull be owned by someone who isn't physically active. Above all, this breed needs activity.

The Pit Bull's Needs

All dogs have some specific needs, and before you add a dog to your life you should look at those needs and see if you will be able to meet them. This could mean the difference between a successful relationship with a dog or the need to give the dog up later.

First of all, your companionship is very important. As

Every Pit Bull has his own personality. Which dog is right for you?

Photo by Robert Pearcy

mentioned earlier, your Pit Bull will need your company. You must be able to spend some time with him every day.

Second, you must be able to keep him active. Do you like to jog or ride a bicycle? Are you willing to take him to the park to play fetch for an hour every day, rain or shine?

Third, are you willing to take the time and effort to train him? Pit Bulls must have good training that establishes their place in the family. An untrained Pit Bull can be a potentially dangerous dog.

Puppies are a lot of work. An adult dog might be a better choice for busy or less active owners.

Photo by Isabelle Francais

Fourth, if you get a puppy, are you willing to socialize him? As a puppy, your Pit Bull must meet other dogs and learn how to play with them. He must also meet people of all ages, sizes, and ethnic backgrounds. A poorly socialized Pit Bull is a potentially dangerous Pit Bull.

Fifth, you will need a yard that is securely fenced and safe for your Pit Bull. Ideally, the fence should be solid so that passersby will not see your dog (keeping him safe from people who tease or might want to steal him) and to reduce his stressful need to watch out for trespassers.

SELECTING THE RIGHT DOG

Male or Female?

There are a lot of myths concerning the personality traits of males and females. Ultimately, it depends more on the personality of each individual dog. Spayed bitches (females) and neutered dogs (males) are usually a little calmer than those that are not. Spaying and neutering removes the sexual hormones and the sexual tension that goes along with the hormones. To be a good pet and companion, your Pit Bull doesn't need those hormones anyway.

Male Pit Bulls are bigger and heavier than females and, as a result, more powerful, too. Females are usually a little lighter in bone structure. A full-grown male Pit Bull is a lot of hard muscle, hard elbows, and rough paws!

Male Pit Bulls tend to be a little more reactive, responding to other canine challenges quicker than bitches, and are often more protective of the house and yard. Females do tend to respond to training better than males. However, these are just generalizations, and individual dogs (and bitches) may vary from these tendencies.

What Age?

All puppies are adorable, especially Pit Bull puppies with their rounded noses, fat tummies, and huge paws. However, puppies are a lot of work. In fact, adding a puppy to your house is much like having a baby in the family. Puppies, just like babies, need to eat, sleep, and relieve themselves often, and, in short, they will demand a lot of your time.

As your puppy grows, he will become a treasured part of your family and, by the time your Pit Bull is grown up (in about three years), he will have become your "best friend."

Raising a puppy is a lot of work and is more than many people are capable of. However, just because a puppy might not be the right dog for you doesn't mean you can't have a wonderful "best friend." There

RESCUE GROUPS
American Pit Bull Terrier breed clubs often run rescue programs for Pit Bulls needing new homes. If you can find a rescue group in your area (call the local shelter or humane society), take advantage of their services. Rescue volunteers prescreen the dogs taken in for adoption as to the dog's physical health, personality, training (or lack thereof), and his ability to get along with other dogs. The dogs are usually spayed or neutered prior to adoption, vaccinated, and given a thorough health exam.

are many adult dogs looking for a good home.

There are some drawbacks to adopting an adult dog. The process can be compared to buying a used car—sometimes you get a gem, sometimes you get a lemon. Unfortunately, a "lemon" Pit Bull could be dangerous.

When you adopt an adult Pit Bull, you may not know what has happened to this dog prior

Photo by Isabelle Francais

Pay attention to body language when you evaluate an adult Pit Bull. A friendly, outgoing dog will be relaxed, smiling, and wagging his tail.

to the adoption. Has he been used for dogfighting? If he has a number of scars on him, that is a real possibility. Has he been badly treated? If he ducks away from your hand or is frightened of the broom, the hose, or a stick, then he probably has been beaten. His past misfortunes can have great bearing on his future behavior.

Newly adopted dogs must be given time to settle into their new home. Some dogs will need months to realize that they are now secure and can relax. A newly adopted Pit Bull may be jumpy and clingy, unable to

allow you out of his sight. Usually these behaviors will decrease as he settles into the new home, bonds with his new owners, and feels more comfortable.

Finding an Adult Dog

You can check for adult Pit Bulls at your local shelter or humane society. Unfortunately, some shelters do not place Pit Bulls for adoption. In some places, all Pit Bulls are euthanized. Call your local shelter or humane society to find out what their policies are regarding Pit Bulls.

Some shelter workers who disagree with these policies do find ways around them, however. Pit Bulls coming into the shelter might be called American Staffordshire Terriers or Bull Terriers. These breeds are different, of course, but if a change in name can save a dog's life, why argue?

Evaluating an Adult Dog

Once you find an adult Pit Bull, how can you tell whether this is the right dog for you? Do you like this dog? The decision should not be entirely emotional, of course, but the relationship won't succeed at all if you don't like the dog. Does the dog like you? He can bond with you later, but if the dog is afraid of you, very leery of you, or doesn't want anything to do with you, that bonding process might never happen.

Do you know why this dog is available for adoption? In Pit Bulls, this is a very important question. Was he tossed out the door by people training dogs to

Because Pit Bulls have such strong personalities, it is important to pick a puppy with a personality that matches yours.

Photo by Isabelle Francais

american pit bull terrier

fight? Maybe he wouldn't fight and they didn't want him anymore. If you think this is farfetched, don't. It happens more often than we know. Was this dog too aggressive for a family with kids? Was he too powerful for a family not willing to spend the time to train him? There are many reasons why a dog might not have stayed in his home, and if you can find out why he was given up, it will help you decide whether he is the right dog for you.

What is this Pit Bull's personality like? Pit Bulls are normally very friendly with people, even strangers, when not in a situation where they feel the need to defend territory or themselves. The dog should be willing to play or be petted. Hopefully, he will even roll over for a tummy rub. However, if he looks at you sideways with a lowered head, be careful, he's worried. If he stands on tiptoes, with his head elevated, and stares you in the eyes, look away and leave that dog alone. He's challenging you and is strong enough to win. Ideally, the dog should be relaxed and should smile, pant, and wag his tail when you talk to him or whistle to him.

Ideally, you should look for a dog that is happy to see you without showing too much worry or fearfulness and no aggression. You want a dog that is housetrained and, preferably, has had some obedience training. Make sure you are willing to live with the dog's behavior problems until you can spend some time training him.

Finding a Puppy

If you have the time, patience, and resources to raise a puppy, you will want to find a reputable American Pit Bull Terrier breeder. Breeder referrals can come from many sources. If you know of a neighbor with an American Pit Bull Terrier with a nice personality, ask her where she got her dog. Your veterinarian might have clients that consistently produce nice, well-mannered Pit Bull puppies. You may want to attend a United Kennel Club (UKC) dog show in your neighborhood and talk to American Pit Bull Terrier owners there.

Once you find a few breeders, make an appointment to meet them. At this meeting, ask the breeder the following questions: "Are you active in dog sports?" If the breeder shows her dogs in UKC conformation dog shows, her dogs are probably good examples of the breed. If she participates in obedience trials, her dogs are trainable. She may also compete in weight-pulling contests or she may volunteer with a therapy dog group, both of which are good activities for the breed.

"Do you belong to any American Pit Bull Terrier breed clubs?" These clubs keep breeders and owners up-to-date on any Pit Bull issues, including health problems and legislation against the breed.

"What health problems have you seen in your dogs?" If she says none, be skeptical. Pit Bulls are normally very healthy dogs, but a line with no health problems whatsoever is rare. Hip dysplasia, allergies, bloat, and a few other problems do occur in the breed. Ask the breeder what she is doing to try and prevent these potential threats.

"Can you provide me with a list of references?" She will give you a list of people that she knows are happy with her dogs, not people who are disgruntled, but that's okay. Ask the people if they are satisfied with their transactions with this breeder. Did she come through with promised paperwork? Is the dog what she promised him to be?

Would they do business with this breeder again?

A caring breeder will ask you as many questions as you ask. She will want to make sure her dogs are not going to dogfighters or research labs. She will want references for you, too. Don't get defensive—she is trying to do the right thing for her dogs. Instead, answer her questions truthfully. If by some chance she says her dogs are not right for you, listen to her. After all, she knows her dogs better than you do.

Evaluating a Puppy

Each puppy has his or her own personality, and finding the right personality to match with yours is sometimes a

When you meet a puppy for the first time, take him somewhere away from his mother and littermates to find out how he will react to you on his own.

Photo by Isabelle Francais

challenge. Because Pit Bulls have such a strong personality, making the wrong match could doom the relationship to failure. For example, if you are an extrovert, are outgoing, happy, and very active, a quiet, withdrawn, submissive puppy would be overwhelmed by you and your household. However, that puppy would be perfect for you if you, too, are quiet and introverted.

When you go look at a litter of puppies, there are a few things you can do to help evaluate the personalities of the various puppies. First, take one puppy into another room away from his mother. Set the puppy on the floor and then walk a few steps away. Squat down and call the puppy to you. An outgoing, extroverted Pit Bull puppy will come right away and try to climb into your lap. If you stand up and walk away, he will be under your feet. If you throw a piece of crumpled paper, he will dash after it and rip it to shreds. This puppy will do well with an owner who is just as outgoing as he is. He will need regular exercise, training to help him learn self-control, and a job to occupy his mind.

A quiet, introverted puppy will come to you when you call but may do a belly crawl or roll over and bare his belly at your feet. He will watch you walk away but may be hesitant to follow. If you toss the paper, he may go after it and pick it up but may be hesitant to bring it back to you. This puppy will need gentle handling, positive training, and a gentle hand to bring out his sweet nature.

These two personalities are the extremes for Pit Bull personalities. Most puppies are somewhere in between these two personality types. Try to find a personality that is most like the traits you like in yourself; don't try to get a puppy that you hope will change you or worse yet, that you feel you can change. It won't happen! Find a puppy that is right for you.

BE CAREFUL

Adding any dog to your family should be a time of anticipation and excitement. But to make it work, it also requires thought, research, and preparation. Without it, the entire process could easily become a nightmare. Make sure the Pit Bull you bring into your family has been well researched and evaluated, that this is the best dog you could find, and that he is a safe choice for your family.

Canine
DEVELOPMENT
Stages

UNDERSTANDING THE DOG-OWNER BOND

Why do you like having a dog? Most people say their joy in owning a dog is the relationship with the dog—a bond that is unlike the relationship with any other pet or even with people. One Pit Bull owner said, "Sheeba never criticizes my clothes and never says I laugh too loud. She loves me just as I am!"

The bond that we have with dogs does not happen automatically. It must be renewed with each puppy. The bond itself is not hereditary, although the tendency to bond is. To understand when and how this bond develops, it's important to understand that your Pit Bull is a dog, not a person in a fuzzy dog suit.

Families and Packs

Most researchers agree that the ancestors of today's dogs were wolves. They disagree on

The bond between a Pit Bull and his owner doesn't happen by itself—it requires love, patience, and good training.

what wolves those ancestors were—either the ancestors to today's gray wolves or perhaps a species of wolf that is now extinct. In any event, wolves are social creatures that live in an extended family pack. The pack might consist of a dominant (alpha) male and a dominant (alpha) female, and these two are usually the only two that breed. There will also be subordinate males and females, juveniles, and puppies. This is a very

Sometimes Pit Bull kisses are welcome and sometimes they definitely aren't! To dogs, human body language is inconsistent and confusing.

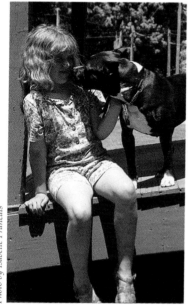

Photo by Isabelle Francais

harmonious group that hunts together, plays together, defends its territory against intruders, and cares for each other. The only discord occurs when there is a change in the pack order. If one of the leaders becomes disabled, an adult leaves the pack, or a subordinate adult tries to assume dominance, there may be some jockeying around to fill that position.

Many experts feel domesticated dogs adapt so well to our lifestyle because we also live in groups. We call our groups families instead of packs, but they are still social groups. However, the comparison isn't really accurate—our families are much more chaotic than the average wolf pack. We are terribly inconsistent with our social rules and rules for behavior. (We let our Pit Bull jump up and paw us when we're in grubby clothes but yell at him when he jumps up on our good clothes.) To the dog, our communication skills are also confusing; our voice says one thing while our body language says something else. To our dogs, we are very complex, confusing creatures. While we can say that both dogs and humans live in social groups and we can use that comparison to understand a little more about our dogs, we must also understand that our families are very different from a wolf pack.

FROM BIRTH TO FOUR WEEKS OF AGE

For the first three weeks of life, the family and the pack are unimportant as far as the Pit Bull puppy is concerned. The only one of any significance is his mother. She is the key to his survival and the source of food, warmth, and security.

At four weeks of age, the Pit Bull puppy's needs are still being met by his mother, but his littermates are becoming more important. His brothers and sisters provide warmth and security when their mother leaves the nest. His curiosity is developing, and he will climb on and over his littermates, learning their scent and feel. During this period, he will learn to use his sense of hearing to follow sounds and his sense of vision to follow moving objects.

His mom will also start disciplining the puppies—very gently, of course—and this early discipline is vitally important to the puppies' future acceptance of discipline and training.

The breeder should be handling the puppies now to get them used to gentle handling by people. The puppies at this age can learn the difference between their mother's touch and a human's touch.

LET THE MOTHER DOG CORRECT

Some inexperienced breeders will stop the mother dog from correcting her puppies, perhaps thinking that the mother dog is impatient, tired, or a poor mother. When the mother dog is not allowed to correct the puppies naturally, the puppies do not learn how to accept discipline and therefore have a hard time later when their new owner tries to establish some rules. Orphaned puppies raised by people suffer from these problems. The mother dog knows instinctively what to do for her babies, and sometimes a correction—a low growl, a bark, or a snap of the teeth—is exactly what is needed. A Pit Bull who does not learn these early lessons is a potentially dangerous dog.

WEEKS FIVE THROUGH SEVEN

The young Pit Bull goes through some tremendous changes between five and seven

Photo by Isabelle Francais

The mother Pit Bull's corrections are very important to her puppies' future acceptance of rules and discipline.

weeks of age. He is learning to recognize people and is starting to respond to individual voices. He is playing more with his littermates, and the wrestling and scuffling teaches each puppy how to get along, how to play, when the play is too rough, when to be submissive, and what to take seriously. His mother's discipline at this stage of development teaches the puppy to accept corrections, training, and affection

The puppies should never be taken from their mother at this stage of development. Puppies taken away now and sent to new homes may have lasting behavior problems. They often have difficulty dealing with other dogs, may have trouble accepting rules and discipline, and may become excessively shy, aggressive, or fearful.

THE EIGHTH WEEK

The eighth week of life is a frightening time for most puppies. Puppies go through several fear periods during

AVOID FEARFUL PEOPLE

Some people think all Pit Bulls are dangerous dogs. Keep your puppy away from these people. Your puppy is learning to be sensitive to the people around him, and fearful people will cause him to worry because he won't understand why they are afraid. If someone is worried about your puppy's breed, don't try to convince them that Pit Bulls are good dogs—you can do that later when your puppy is safe at home. Just take your puppy away and let him visit with friendly people.

their maturation, and this is the first one. Even though this is the traditional time for most puppies to go to their new homes, they would actually benefit by staying with their littermates for one more week. If the puppy leaves the breeder's home during this fear period and is frightened by the car ride home, he may retain that fear of car rides for the rest of his life. In fact, this stress is why so many puppies get carsick. The same applies to the

Never play rough with your Pit Bull puppy. If he learns to bite playfully now, he could cause accidental injury when he's fully grown.

Photo by Isabelle Francais

american pit bull terrier

puppy's new home, his first trip to the veterinarian's office, or anything else that frightens him.

WEEKS NINE THROUGH TWELVE

The baby Pit Bull can go to his new home anytime during the ninth and tenth weeks of life. At this age, he is ready to form permanent relationships. Take advantage of this and spend time with your new puppy, playing with him and encouraging him to explore his new world. Teach him his name by calling him in a happy voice that is higher pitched than normal. Encourage him to follow you by backing away from him, patting your leg, and calling his name.

CONTROL PLAYTIMES

When you are introducing your puppy to people, don't let them play rough with him. Because Pit Bulls are tough, strong dogs, some people think that all play should be rough and tumble, and it shouldn't be. You want to teach your puppy to be gentle with people, not rough. Control the games and take your puppy out of any situation where people are being too rough.

RETRIEVING

Begin retrieving games at 9 to 12 weeks of age. Get your Pit Bull's attention with a toy he likes, and then toss it four to six feet away. When he grabs the toy, call him back to you in a happy tone of voice. Praise him enthusiastically when he brings it back to you. If he runs away and tries to get you to chase him, stand up and walk away, stopping the game completely. Don't chase him! Let him learn now, while he's young, that he must play the games by your rules. Chasing a ball or soft flying disc can be great exercise for the puppy, and teaching him to play by your rules sets the stage for a sound working relationship later.

Socialization is very important now, too. Socialization is more than simply introducing your puppy to other people, dogs, noises, and places. It is making sure that your puppy is not frightened by these things as you introduce them. For example, once your baby Pit Bull has had some vaccinations (check with your veterinarian), take your puppy with you to the pet store when you go to buy dog food. While there, introduce your puppy to the store clerks, other customers, and even to the store parrot. Your trip there could also include walking up some stairs, walking on slippery floors, and going through an automatic door. All of these things, introduced gradually and with encouragement, and repeated all over town (on different days, of course) add up to a confident, well-socialized puppy.

During this stage of development, your Pit Bull puppy's pack instincts are developing. He is beginning to understand which people belong to his pack (or family) and which do not. Do not let him growl at visitors during this stage; he is much too young to understand when and how to protect. Instead, stop the growling and let him know that you—as his pack leader—can protect the family.

You can show him his position in the family in several different ways, but one of the easiest ways is to lay him down, roll him over, and give him a tummy rub. This exercise may seem very simple, but by baring his tummy he is assuming a submissive position to you. When his mother corrected him by growling or barking at him, he would roll over and bare his tummy to her, in essence telling her, "Okay! I understand, you're the boss!" When you have him roll over for a tummy rub, you are helping him understand the same message but you are doing it in a very gentle, loving way.

During this stage of development, discipline is very important. Love, affection, and security are still important, but right now your Pit Bull puppy needs to learn that his life is governed by some rules. Don't allow him to do anything now that you won't want him to continue doing later as a full-grown dog.

WEEKS THIRTEEN THROUGH SIXTEEN

From 13 through 16 weeks of age, your Pit Bull puppy will be trying to establish his position in your family pack. If you were able to set some rules in earlier stages of development, this won't be quite so difficult. However, if you cave in to that adorable puppy face, well, this could be a challenging time!

Consistency in enforcing household rules is very important now, and everyone in the family or household should be enforcing the rules the same way. Pit Bulls are very perceptive, and if your puppy senses a weak link in the chain of command, he will take advantage of it. This doesn't mean he's a bad puppy, it simply means he's a smart puppy.

Dominant personality puppies may start mounting behavior to small children in the family or to the puppy's toys. Obviously, this is undesirable behavior and should be stopped immediately—just don't let it happen!

Socialization to other people, friendly dogs, and other experiences should continue throughout this stage of development.

WEEKS SEVENTEEN THROUGH TWENTY-SIX

Sometime between 17 and 26 weeks of age, most puppies go through another fear period, much like the one they went through at 8 weeks of age. Things the puppy had accepted as normal may suddenly become frightening. A friend's Pit Bull walked into the backyard and began barking fearfully at the picnic table that had been there in the same spot since before the puppy joined the family. It was as if the puppy had never noticed it before, and all at once it was very scary!

As your puppy grows, he may pass through several fear stages, during which familiar things may frighten him. As long as you do not reinforce these fears, they will quickly dissipate.

Photo by Isabelle Francais

american pit bull terrier

Make sure you don't reinforce any of these fears. If you pet the puppy or cuddle him and tell him softly, "It's okay, sweetie, don't be afraid," he will assume that these are positive reinforcements for his fears. In other words, your puppy will think he was right to be afraid. Instead, walk up to whatever is scaring him and let him see you touch it as you tell him, "Look at this!" in a happy tone of voice. Use a happy, fun, playful tone of voice so that he can see the thing he is afraid of really isn't scary at all.

Your Pit Bull's protective instincts will continue to develop through this stage. If your Pit Bull continues to show protectiveness or aggression (with growling, snarling, barking, or raised hackles), interrupt his behavior by turning him away or distracting him. If you encourage this behavior this early, or if you correct it too harshly, you will put too much emphasis on it, and your puppy may continue to do it. Too much emphasis this young may result in overprotectiveness or fearfulness in your dog as he grows up. Instead, react with calmness and just stop it from happening.

Pit Bulls are naturally protective as adults, and if you wanted a Pit Bull for this trait, don't worry about interrupting the behavior now. This training will not hamper those instincts. At this age, your Pit Bull puppy doesn't know what or when to protect. Instead of letting him take over (and learn bad habits), stop his behavior and let him know you are in charge. Later, when he's more mature, you can encourage the specific protectiveness you want.

THE TEENAGE MONTHS

The teenage months in dogs are very much like the teenage years in human children. Human teenagers are feeling strong and are striving to prove their ability to take care of themselves. They want to be independent, yet they still want the security of home. These two conflicting needs seem to drive some teens (and their parents) absolutely crazy.

Dogs can be very much the same way. Pit Bulls in adolescence push the boundaries of their rules,

Photo by Isabelle Francais

Previously well-behaved "teenage" dogs may test their owner's authority—for example, by jumping up on people or playing too roughly. Consistent enforcement of household rules during this stage is necessary.

trying to see if you really will enforce those rules. Most Pit Bull owners say their dogs in this stage of growing up act "too full of themselves."

The teenage stage in Pit Bulls usually hits at about 12 months of age, although it's not unusual to see it happen a month or two earlier. You'll know when it happens. One day you will ask your previously well-trained dog to do something he knows very well, such as sit, and he'll look at you as if he's never heard that word before in his life, and even if he had, he still wouldn't do it.

Other common behaviors include a regression in social skills. Your previously well-socialized Pit Bull may start barking at other dogs or jumping on people. He may start getting rough with children or chasing the cat.

During this stage of development, you need to consistently enforce social and household rules. Hopefully, you will have started obedience training already, because that control will help. If you haven't started obedience training, do so now—don't wait any longer.

Make sure, too, that your dog regards you as the leader. This is not the time to try and be best friends—that would

Photo by Isabelle Francais

Even your grown-up Pit Bull will sometimes want to clown around.

american pit bull terrier

cause a dominant personality to regard you as weak. Instead, act like the leader. Stand tall when you relate to your dog. Bend over him (not down to him) when you pet him. You should always go first through doorways or up the stairs, making him wait and follow you. You should always eat first before you feed him.

As the leader, you can give him permission to do things. For example, if he goes to pick up a toy for you to throw for him, give him permission to do it, "Good boy to bring me your toy!" If he lies down at your feet (by his own choice) tell him, "Good boy to lie down!" By giving him permission and praising him, you are putting yourself in control, even though he was already doing it of his own accord.

You need to understand that this rebellion is not aimed at you, personally. Your Pit Bull is not doing this to you. Instead, it is a very natural part of growing up. Keep in mind that this, too, shall pass. Your Pit Bull will grow up someday. Adolescence usually only lasts a few months (in dogs, anyway).

GROWING UP

Pit Bulls are not usually considered fully mentally and physically mature until they are three years old. And even then, some Pit Bulls still act like a puppy behaviorally for even longer. Usually, the bitches (females) act mature a little earlier than the males.

After the teenage stage but before maturity, your Pit Bull may go through another fear period. This usually hits at about 14 months of age but may be later. Handle this one just like you did the others; don't reinforce your dog's fears. Happily, this is usually the last fear stage your dog will have.

There may be another period of challenging—seeing if you really are the boss—at about two years of age. Treat this as you did the teenage stage: Enforce the rules and praise what he does right.

When your Pit Bull reaches his third birthday, throw a party. He is usually considered grown up now. However, "grown up" to a Pit Bull doesn't always mean life is serious. It will be when situations demand it, but in the meantime, life for a Pit Bull is fun!

Early
PUPPY
Training

A young puppy's mind is like a brand new computer hard drive. It is basically empty except for the instincts the puppy was born with and what his mother taught him before he left her. What you teach your Pit Bull puppy in his early months will have bearing on the puppy's behavior for the rest of his life.

Therefore, it's important to keep in mind a vision of what your Pit Bull will grow up to be. Although Pit Bulls are medium-sized dogs (not giant breeds), many do get quite large. They are strong, powerful dogs, and you need to keep this in mind. At ten weeks of age, your Pit Bull puppy will enjoy a cuddle on your lap, but will you still

Your new Pit Bull puppy's mind is a blank slate—teach him now what you want him to know as an adult.

Photo by Isabelle Francais

want him to do that when he's 60 pounds of muscle and hard elbows? Teach him as a puppy what you want him to do as an adult.

HOUSEHOLD RULES

It's important to start teaching your Pit Bull puppy the household rules that you wish him to observe as soon as possible. Your eight- to ten-week-old puppy is not too

A Pit Bull puppy may be a good lap dog, but a 60-pound adult Pit Bull will be a little overwhelming! Consistent rules from the start will make life easier for both of you.

young to learn, and by starting early, you can prevent him from learning bad habits.

When deciding what rules you want him to learn, look at your Pit Bull puppy, not as the baby he is now, but as the adult he will grow up to be. Are you going to want him up on the furniture when he's fully grown? Do you want him to jump up on the neighbor's children or your grandmother?

Some rules you may want to institute could include teaching your Pit Bull that jumping on people is not allowed, he must behave when guests come to the house, he should stay out of the kitchen, he should leave the trash cans alone, and he should chew only on his toys.

Teaching your Pit Bull puppy these rules is not difficult. Be very clear with your corrections. When he does something wrong, correct him using a deep, firm tone of voice, "No jump!" When he does something right, use a higher-pitched tone of voice, "Good boy to chew on your toy!" You must be very clear—either something is right or it is wrong, there are no shades of gray in between.

ACCEPTING THE LEASH

Learning to accept the leash can be difficult for some

puppies. If your Pit Bull puppy learns to dislike the leash as a young puppy, he may continue to resent it for many years. However, if he learns that the leash is a key to more exciting things, he will welcome the leash.

Soon after you bring your puppy home, put a soft buckle collar on his neck. Make sure it's loose enough to come over his head if he gets tangled up in something. Give him a day or two to get used to the collar. Then, when you are going to be close by and can supervise him, snap the leash onto the collar and let him drag it behind him. As he walks around, he will step on the leash, feel it tug on his neck and, in doing so, will get used to the feel of it.

After two or three short sessions like this, you can then teach your puppy to follow you on the leash. Have a few pieces of an easily chewable, soft treat that your puppy enjoys. Hold the leash in one hand and the treats in another. Show him the treat and back away a few steps as you tell your puppy, "Let's go! Good boy!" When he follows you a few steps, praise him and give him the treat. Pit Bull puppies are usually very food-motivated, and when he learns that a treat is being

Photo by Isabelle Francais

If your Pit Bull learns that his leash is the ticket to fun outdoor adventures, he won't dislike it. A gradual introduction to both the collar and leash will help.

offered, he should follow you with no problem.

Repeat this two or three times and then stop the training session. Reward your puppy by giving him a tummy rub or by throwing the ball a few times.

After two or three training sessions like this, make it more challenging by backing up slowly or faster or by making turns. If he gets confused or balks, make it simple again until he's willingly following you again.

IF YOUR PUPPY BALKS

If your puppy balks, do not use the leash to drag him to you. This will cause him to dig his feet in and apply the brakes. Instead, kneel down, open your arms wide, and encourage him to come to you, "Hey, Sweetie, here! Good boy!" When he dashes to your lap, praise him and tell him what a wonderful puppy he is. Then try the exercise again

INTRODUCING THE CAR

Many puppies are afraid of the car because a ride in the car was the first strange thing to happen to them when taken from their mother and littermates. The car also takes them to the veterinarian's office, another strange place where someone in a white coat pokes them, prods them, and gives them shots. You don't want this fear of the car to grab hold, though. You want your puppy to understand that riding in the car is something fun to do.

Start by lifting your puppy into the car and handing him a treat. As soon as he finishes the treat, lift him down and

This Pit Bull clearly thinks that car rides are great! Remember to use a crate or special doggie seatbelt in the car to make sure your road trips are safe as well as fun.

Photo by Isabelle Francais

walk him away. Repeat this simple exercise several times a day for a few days. Then lift him into the car, give him a treat, let him eat it, and then let him explore the car for a few minutes. After he has sniffed for a few minutes, give him another treat, let him eat it, then lift him down and walk away. Continue this training for a week or two, depending on how nervous your puppy is in the car.

When your puppy is expecting a treat in the car, put his crate in the car (we'll talk more about crates later in this chapter) and strap it down securely. Put your puppy in his crate, give him a treat, and then start the car's engine. Back down the driveway and then back up to the house. Stop the engine, give your puppy a treat, and let him out of his crate and the car.

The next time, drive down the street and then back. Then go around the block. Increase the distances and times of the drives very gradually. Keep in mind that you want your puppy to expect good things in the car, not scary things. Your Pit Bull puppy will have a lifetime of car rides ahead of him, and life will be much nicer if he enjoys the rides.

END ON A HIGH NOTE
Always end these (and all) training sessions on a high note. If your Pit Bull puppy is worried, scared, and confused, help him do something right and then end the training session with that praise. Never end the session at a negative point in the training or it will affect his outlook toward training later.

SOCIAL HANDLING

Your Pit Bull puppy cannot care for himself. You must be able to brush and comb him, bathe him, check his feet for cuts and scrapes, and clean his ears. Your Pit Bull puppy doesn't understand why you need to do these things that annoy him, and he may struggle when you try to care for him. This social handling exercise will help teach your puppy to accept your care:

Sit down on the floor with your puppy and have him lie down between your legs. He can lie on his back or on his side—let him get comfortable. Start by giving him a slow, easy tummy rub. The idea here is to relax him. If your movements are fast and vigorous, you'll make him want to play. Keep it slow and gentle. If he starts to struggle, tell him calmly, "Easy. Be still." Restrain him gently if you need to do so.

When your puppy is relaxed, start giving him a massage. Start at his neck and ears, gently rubbing all around the base of each ear and working down the neck to the shoulders. Continue over his body, gently massaging it, while at the same time you check his body for cuts, scratches, lumps, bumps, bruises, fleas, ticks, or any other problems that need to be taken care of.

Once your puppy has learned to enjoy this handling

When your puppy is thoroughly relaxed, it is easier to groom and care for him.

Photo by Isabelle Francais

SOCIAL HANDLING

Pit Bulls are very strong, powerful dogs. If you need to clean your dog's ears, you cannot have him struggle against you, using his strength against yours. You would never be able to care for him. Therefore, it is very important that he learns at a young age to tolerate any necessary handling. Practice the social handling exercise often.

you can clean his ears, wash out his eyes, trim his toenails, or do anything else that needs doing during the massage.

Relax!

You can also use the social handling exercise to relax your puppy when he's overstimulated. If you let him in from the backyard and he's full of high-octane Pit Bull energy, don't chase him down or try to correct him. Instead, sit down on the floor and invite him to join you. (Use a treat to get him to come to you if he needs some extra incentive.) Once he's come to you, lay him down and begin the massage. He will relax and calm down, and in the process, you are also giving him the attention he needs from you.

THE PROCESS OF HOUSETRAINING

Crate Training

By about five weeks of age, most puppies are starting to toddle away from their mom and littermates to relieve themselves. You can use this instinct to keep the bed clean, and with the help of a crate, you can housetrain your Pit Bull puppy.

A crate is a plastic or wire travel cage that you can use as your Pit Bull's bed. Many new Pit Bull owners shudder at the thought of putting their puppy in a cage. "I could never do that," they say. "It would be like putting my children in jail!" A puppy is not a child, however, and he has different needs and instincts. Puppies like to curl up in small, dark places. That's why they like to sleep under the coffee table or under a chair.

Because your Pit Bull puppy has an instinct to keep his bed clean, being confined in the crate will help develop more bowel and bladder control. When he is confined for gradually extended periods of time, he will hold his wastes to avoid soiling his bed. It is your responsibility to make sure he isn't left in the crate too long.

The crate will also be your Pit Bull puppy's place of refuge. If he's tired, hurt, or sick, allow him to go back to his crate to sleep or hide. If he's overstimulated or excited, put him back in his crate to calm down. "Time outs" are a wonderful training tool for puppies, including easily stimulated, active, young Pit Bulls.

Because the crate physically confines the puppy, it can also prevent some unwanted behaviors, such as destructive

Not only does the crate aid in housetraining, but it is a good place for overstimulated puppies to calm down.

Photo by Isabelle Francais

chewing or raiding the trash cans. When you cannot supervise the puppy or when you leave the house, put him in his crate and he won't be able to get into trouble.

Introducing the Crate

Introduce your puppy to the crate by propping open the door and tossing a treat inside. As you do this, tell your puppy, "Go to bed!" Let him go inside to get the treat. Let him investigate the crate and come and go as he wishes. When he's comfortable with that, offer him his next meal in the crate. Once he's in, close the door behind him. Let him out when he's through eating. Offer several meals in the same fashion to show your puppy that the crate is a pretty neat place.

After your Pit Bull puppy is used to going in and out for treats and meals, start feeding him in the normal location again, and go back to offering a treat for going into the crate. Tell him, "Sweetie, go to bed," and then give him his treat.

Don't let your puppy out of the crate for a temper tantrum. If he starts crying, screaming, throwing himself at the door, or scratching at the door, correct him verbally, "No, quiet!" or simply close the door to the room and walk away. If you let him out for a tantrum, you will teach him that temper tantrums work. Instead, let him out when you are ready to let him out and when he is quiet.

Crate Location

The ideal place for the crate is in your bedroom, within arm's reach of the bed. This will give your Pit Bull eight uninterrupted hours with you while you do nothing but sleep. In these busy times, that is quality time!

Having you nearby will give your Pit Bull puppy a feeling of security, whereas exiling him to the laundry room or backyard will isolate him. He will be more apt to cry, whine, chew destructively, or get into other trouble because of loneliness and fear.

Having the crate close at night will save you some wear and tear, too. If he needs to go outside during the night (and he may need to for a few weeks) you will hear him whine and you can let him out before he has an accident. If he's restless or bored, you can rap on the top of his crate and tell him to be quiet without getting out of bed.

Photo by Isabelle Francais

Don't just open the door and send your puppy out by himself to eliminate. Go outside with him and praise him for going in the right place.

Housetraining

One of the most common methods of housetraining a puppy is paper training. The puppy is taught to relieve himself on newspapers and then, at some point, is retrained to go outside. Paper training teaches the puppy to relieve himself in the house. Is that really what you want your Pit Bull to know?

Teach your Pit Bull what you want him to know now and later as an adult. Take him outside to the place where you want him to relieve himself and tell him, "Go potty." (Use any word you'll be comfortable saying.) When he has done what it is he needs to do, praise him.

Don't just open the door and send your puppy outside. How do you know that he has relieved himself? Go out with him so that you can teach him the command, praise him when he does it, and know when he is done and it's safe to let him back inside.

If he doesn't relieve himself when you take him outside, just put him back in his crate for a little while and take him back outside later. Do NOT let him run around the house—even supervised—if he has not relieved himself outside.

Successful housetraining is based on setting your Pit Bull puppy up for success rather than failure. Keep accidents to a minimum and praise him when he does relieve himself appropriately.

PUNISHMENT

Do not try to housetrain your puppy by correcting him for relieving himself in the house. If you scold him or rub his nose in his mess, you are not teaching him *where* he needs to relieve himself; you are, instead, teaching him that you think going potty is wrong. Because he has to go, he will then become sneaky about it, and you will find puddles and piles in strange places. Keep in mind that the act of relieving himself is very natural. He has to do this. So instead of concentrating on correction, emphasize praise for going in the right place.

Establish a Routine

Pit Bulls, like many other dogs, are creatures of habit and thrive on a routine. Housetraining is much easier if there is a set routine for eating, eliminating, playing, walking, training, and sleeping. A workable schedule might look like this:

• **6:00 am**—Dad wakes up and takes the puppy outside. After the puppy relieves himself, Dad praises him and brings him inside. Dad fixes the puppy's breakfast, offers him water, and then sends him out in the backyard while Dad goes to take his shower.

• **7:00 am**—Sister goes outside to play with the puppy for a few minutes before getting ready for school. Just before she leaves, she brings the puppy inside, puts him in his crate, and gives him a treat.

• **11:00 am**—A dog-loving neighbor who is retired comes over. He lets the puppy out of his crate and takes him outside. The neighbor is familiar with the puppy's training, so he praises the puppy when he relieves himself. He throws the ball for the puppy, pets him, and cuddles him. When the puppy is worn out, he puts him back in his crate and gives him a treat.

• **3:00 pm**—Sister comes home from school and takes the puppy outside. She

THERE ARE NO ACCIDENTS

If the puppy relieves himself in the house, it is not his fault, it's yours. That means the puppy was not supervised well enough or he wasn't taken outside in time. The act of relieving himself is very natural to the puppy, and the idea that there are certain areas where relieving himself is not acceptable is foreign to him. His instincts tell him to keep his bed clean, but that's all. We need to teach him where we want him to go and to prevent him from going in other places. That requires supervision on your part.

throws the ball for the puppy, cleans up the yard, and then takes the puppy for a walk. When they get back, she brings the puppy to her bedroom while she does her homework.

• **6:00 pm**—Mom takes the puppy outside to go potty, praises him, and then feeds him dinner.

• **8:00 pm**—After Brother plays with the puppy, he brushes him and then takes him outside to go potty.

• **11:00 pm**—Dad takes the puppy outside for one last trip before bed.

The schedule you set up will have to work with your normal routine and lifestyle. Just keep in mind that your Pit Bull puppy should not remain in the crate for longer than three to four hours at a time except during the night. In addition, the puppy will need to relieve himself after waking up, after eating, after playtime, and every three to four hours in between.

Limit the Puppy's Freedom

Many puppies do not want to take the time to go outside

Pit Bull puppies thrive on a set routine for eating, eliminating, playing, walking, training, and sleeping.

Photo by Isabelle Francais

american pit bull terrier

THINK ABOUT TIMING

Do you walk your dog when he has to go potty? Many dog owners live in condos and apartments, and the dog must go for a walk to relieve himself. These dogs often learn that the walk is over once they go potty, so they hold it as long as possible so that the walk continues. To avoid this trap, encourage your puppy to relieve himself right away, praise him, and then continue the walk or outing for a little while afterward.

to relieve themselves because everything exciting happens in the house. After all, that's where all the family members

PATIENCE, PATIENCE, AND MORE PATIENCE

Pit Bull puppies need time to develop bowel and bladder control. Establish a routine that seems to work well for you and your puppy and then stick to it. Give your puppy time to learn what you want and time to grow up. If you stick to the schedule, your puppy will progress. However, don't let success go to your head. A few weeks without a mistake doesn't mean your Pit Bull puppy is housetrained, it means your routine is working! Too much freedom too soon will result in problems.

are. If your Pit Bull puppy is like this, you will find him sneaking off somewhere—behind the sofa or to another room—to relieve himself. By limiting the puppy's freedom, you can prevent some of these mistakes. Close bedroom doors and use baby gates across hallways to keep him close. If you can't keep an eye on him, put him in his crate or outside.

Have patience with your Pit Bull puppy. Remember that he is only a baby and, like a human infant, will need time to learn new things.

Photo by Isabelle Francais

The Basic
OBEDIENCE
Commands

ALL PIT BULLS NEED TRAINING

When you combine strong, muscular dogs with intelligence and curiosity, you can see why all Pit Bulls need training. Pit Bulls are simply too full of themselves not to be trained. Their curiosity, sense of fun, protectiveness, and flat-out brute strength would get them into entirely too much trouble.

THE TEACHING PROCESS

Although Pit Bulls are a very intelligent breed, you cannot simply tell your Pit Bull to do something and expect him to understand your verbal language. Training is a process that begins with teaching that certain words have meanings and that you would like him to follow your directions. Your Pit Bull, however, doesn't

Pit Bulls are too strong, powerful, and smart to go without training. Good training will ensure a well-mannered, obedient pet.

Many Pit Bull owners don't admit their dog needs training. "He does everything I ask," they say. Yet when asked specific questions about behavior, the answer changes. A trained Pit Bull won't jump up on people, dash out the open door, or raid the trash can.

Dog owners benefit from training, too. During training, you learn how to teach your Pit Bull and how to motivate him to be good so that you can encourage good behavior. You also learn how to prevent problem behavior from happening and how to correct mistakes that do happen.

Photo by Isabelle Francais

american pit bull terrier

understand why you want him to do these things; after all, why should he come when you call him? There might be something he would rather do at that particular moment. He doesn't know why these commands are so important to you. Therefore, training is a process.

Show Your Dog

First of all, you want to show your dog what it is you want him to do and that there is a word—a human spoken sound— associated with that action or position. For example, when teaching him to sit, you can help him into position as you tell him, "Sweetie, sit." Follow that with praise—"Good boy to sit!"—even if you helped him into position.

You will follow a similar pattern when teaching your dog most new things. If you want him to get off the sofa, you can tell him, "Sweetie, off the furniture," as you take him by the collar and pull him off. When he's off the furniture, tell him, "Good boy to get off the furniture."

Praise

Praise him every time he does something right even if you help him do it. Your Pit Bull will pay more attention and try harder if he is praised for his efforts. However, don't praise him when

it's undeserved. Pit Bulls are very intelligent dogs and will quickly figure this out. Instead, give enthusiastic praise when he makes an effort and does something right for you.

Correct

Do not correct your dog until he understands what it is you want him to do. After he understands and is willing to obey the command, and then chooses NOT to do it, you may correct him with a verbal correction, "Sweetie, no!" or a quick snap and release of the collar. Use only as much correction as is needed to get his attention and no more. With corrections, less is usually better as long as your dog is responding.

Your Timing

The timing of your praise, corrections, and interruptions is very important. Praise him as he is doing something right. Correct him when he makes the mistake. Interrupt him as he starts to stick his nose into the trash can. If your timing is slow, he may not understand what you are trying to teach him.

Be Fair

Pit Bulls resent corrections that are too harsh or unfair. They will show this resentment by refusing to work, by planting themselves and refusing to move, or by fighting back. Never, ever push a Pit Bull to the point that he tries to fight back. If you do, there is too great a chance that you will lose that fight. In addition, it's a poor dog training technique and unnecessary.

USE INTERRUPTIONS

Interrupt incorrect behavior as you see it happen. If your dog is walking by the kitchen trash can and turns to sniff it, interrupt him, "Leave it alone!" If you tell him to sit and he does sit, but then starts to get up, interrupt him, "No! Sit." By interrupting him, you can stop incorrect behavior before or as it happens.

Interruptions and corrections alone will not teach your Pit Bull. They are used to stop, at that moment, undesirable behavior or actions. Your Pit Bull learns much more when you reward good behavior. Stop the behavior you don't want, but lavishly praise the actions you want to continue.

THE BASIC COMMANDS

Come

The come command is one of the most important commands your Pit Bull needs to learn. Not only is the come command important around the house in your daily routine, but it could also be a lifesaver someday, especially if he should decide to dash into the street when a car is coming. Because the come command is so important, you

Always call your Pit Bull to come with an enthusiastic gesture and a high-pitched tone of voice.

will use two different techniques to teach your dog to come to you when you call him.

Come with a Treat

The first technique will use a sound stimulus and a treat to teach your Pit Bull to come when you call him. Take a small plastic container, such as a margarine tub, and put a handful of dry dog food in it. Put the lid on and shake it. It should make a nice rattling sound.

USING A SOUND STIMULUS

Do you remember those silent dog whistles that used to be advertised in comic books? There was nothing magical about those whistles, except that they were so high-pitched dogs could hear them but people couldn't. The container we're using for teaching the come command works on the same principal that the silent dog whistle used: It's a sound stimulus you can use to get the dog's attention so that you can teach him. By teaching him to pay attention to the sound of the shaker, and by teaching him that the sound of the shaker means he's going to get a treat, we can make coming when called that much more exciting. Your dog will be more likely to come to you, especially when there are distractions, if he's excited about it.

Have the shaker in one hand and some good dog treats in the other. Shake the container, and as your Pit Bull looks at it and you, ask him, "Sweetie, cookie?" Use whatever word he already knows means treat. When you say "cookie," pop a treat in his mouth. Do it again. Shake, shake, say "Sweetie, cookie?" and pop a treat in his mouth.

The sound of the container, your verbal question, and the treat are all becoming associated in his mind. He is learning that the sound of the container equals the treat, an important lesson. Do this several times a day for several days.

Then, with him sitting in front of you, replace the word "cookie" with the word "come." Shake the container, say "Sweetie, come!" and pop a treat in his mouth. You are rewarding him even though he didn't actually come to you—he is still sitting in front of you. However, you are teaching him that the sound of the shaker now equals the word "come," and he still gets the treat. Another important lesson. Practice this several times a day for several days.

When your Pit Bull is happy to hear the shaker and is drooling to get a treat, start calling him across the room. Shake the container as you say, "Sweetie, come!" When he dashes to you, continue to give him a treat as you praise him, "Good boy to come!" Practice this up and down the hallway, inside and outside, and across the backyard. Make it fun, keeping up with the treats and the verbal praise.

DON'T WORRY

Some people have reservations about this technique because they are worried that the dog will not come to them when they don't have a treat. First of all, you will use two different techniques to teach the come command, and only one technique uses the treats. Second, even with this technique, you will eventually stop using treats. However, by using this technique when first introducing the come command, you can produce such a strong, reliable response, it's worth all of your efforts.

DON'T USE THE COME COMMAND TO PUNISH

Never call your dog to come and then punish him for something he did earlier. Not only is the late punishment ineffective (it always is), but that unfair punishment will teach your dog to avoid you when you call him. Keep the come command positive.

Photo by Isabelle Francais

Treats are great training tools, even after you stop using them. Using food rewards at first to teach new commands creates a strong, permanent motivation for the dog to obey.

The Come with a Long Line

The second method used to teach your dog to come uses a long leash or a length of clothesline rope. Because Pit Bulls are athletic and fast, have a line at least 30 feet in length. Fasten the line to your Pit Bull's collar, and then let him go play. When he is distracted by something, call him with, "Sweetie, come!" If he responds and comes right away, praise him.

If he doesn't respond right away, do *not* call him again. Pick up the line, back away from

The long line method teaches your dog to come without a food reward. Attach the line to his collar and call his name. If he doesn't respond, pull him to you.

him, and, using the line, make him come to you. Do not give him a verbal correction at this time, because he may associate the verbal correction with coming to you. Instead, simply make him come to you even if you have to drag him in with the line.

Let him go again, and repeat the entire exercise. Make sure you always praise him when he does decide to come to you. If he is really distracted, use the shaker and treats along with the long line, especially in the early stages of training. You can

always wean him from the treats later, but the immediate goal is to make the come command work.

Sit and Release

When your Pit Bull learns to sit and sit still, he learns to control himself and that there are consequences to his actions. Learning to control himself, thereby controlling the consequences to his actions, is a very big lesson. The sit is also a good alternative action for problem behavior. Your Pit Bull cannot both sit still *and* jump

BE CAUTIOUS

Don't allow your Pit Bull to have freedom off the leash until he is grown up enough to handle the responsibility and is very well trained. Many dog owners let their dog off leash much too soon, and the dogs learn bad habits their owners wish they hadn't learned. Each time your dog learns that he can ignore or run away from you, it reinforces the fact that he can. Instead, let him run around and play while dragging the long line. That way you can always regain control when you need it.

you move your right hand (with the treats) from his nose over his head toward his tail. He will lift his head to watch your hand. As his head goes up and back, his hips will go down. As he sits, praise him, "Good boy to sit!" and give him a treat. Pet him in the sitting position.

When you are ready for him to get up, tap him on the shoulder as you tell him, "Release!" Each exercise needs a beginning and an end. The sit command is the beginning, and the release command tells him

Don't allow your Pit Bull off leash unless he is very well trained—you never know what he might get himself into!

Photo by Isabelle Francais

on you. Learning to sit still for praise can replace jumping up on people for attention. He can't knock his food bowl out of your hand if he's sitting still, waiting patiently for his dinner. You can fasten his leash to his collar more easily if he's sitting still. This is a practical, useful command.

There are two basic methods of teaching your Pit Bull to sit. Some dogs do better with one technique than the other, so try both and see which is better for your Pit Bull.

Hold your Pit Bull's leash in your left hand and have some treats in your right hand. Tell your Pit Bull, "Sweetie, sit!" as he is done and can move now. If he doesn't get up on his own, use your hands on his collar to walk him forward.

If your Pit Bull is too excited by the treats to think, (and some Pit Bulls are like that) put the treats away. Tell your Pit Bull to sit as you place one hand under his chin on the front of the neck, sliding the other hand down his hips to tuck under his back legs. Gently shape him into a sit as you give

SIT, PLEASE!

Once your Pit Bull understands the sit command and is responding well, start having him sit for things that he wants. Have him sit before you hook his leash to his collar before a walk. Have him sit before you give him a treat, give him his meals, or throw his ball. Pit Bulls are a working dog, and sitting can be your Pit Bull's first job.

him the command, "Sweetie, sit." Praise him and release him.

If your dog is wiggly as you try and teach this exercise, keep your hands on him. If he pops up, interrupt that action with a deep, firm tone of voice, "Be still!" When he responds and stops wiggling, praise him quietly and gently.

ONE COMMAND

Don't keep repeating any command. The command is not, "Sit! Sit, sit, sit, please sit. SIT!!" If you give repeated commands to sit, your Pit Bull will assume that carries over to everything else. Tell him one time to sit and then help him do it.

Down

The down exercise continues one of the lessons the sit command started, that of self-control. It is hard for many energetic, bouncy, young Pit Bulls to control their own actions, but it is a lesson all must learn.

Tell your dog one time to sit and then shape him into the sit position if necessary, without repeating the command.

Practicing the down exercise teaches your Pit Bull to lie down and be still.

Start with your Pit Bull in a sit. Rest one hand gently on his shoulder and have a treat in the other hand. Let him smell the treat and then tell him, "Sweetie, down," taking the treat straight down to the ground in front of his front paws. As he follows the treat down, use your hand on his shoulders to encourage him to lie down. Praise him, give him the treat, and then have him hold the position for a moment. Then release him in the same way you did from the sit: Pat him on the shoulder, tell him "Release!" and let him get up.

If your dog looks at the treat as you make the signal but doesn't follow the treat to the ground, simply scoop his front legs up and forward as you lay him down. The rest of the exercise is the same.

As your Pit Bull learns what the down command means, you can have him hold it for a few minutes longer before you release him, but do not step away from him yet. Stay next to him, and if he's wiggly, keep a hand on his shoulder to help him stay in position.

Teach the down command using a treat, a verbal command, and a hand gesture toward the ground.

american pit bull terrier

BE FAIR

Make sure you make it very clear to your dog what you want him to do. Remember, something is either right or wrong to your dog; it's not partly right or partly wrong. Be fair with your commands, your praise, and your corrections.

Once each day, have your Pit Bull lie down and then, before you release him, roll him over for a tummy rub. He will enjoy the tummy rub, relax a little, and will learn to enjoy the

The stay command uses an open-palmed hand gesture toward the dog's face, as well as the verbal command.

down position. This is especially important for young Pit Bulls who want to do anything *but* lie down and hold still.

Stay

When your Pit Bull understands both the sit and down commands, you can introduce him to the stay exercise. You want to convey to your Pit Bull that the word "stay" means "hold still." When your dog is sitting and you tell him to stay, you want him to remain in the sitting position until you go back to him and release him. When you tell him to stay while he's lying down, you want him to remain lying down until you go back to him to release him from that position. Eventually, he will be able to hold the sit position for several minutes and the down for even longer.

Start by having your Pit Bull sit. With the leash in your left hand, use it to put a slight bit of pressure backward (toward his tail) as you tell him, "Sweetie, stay." At the same time, use your right hand to give your dog a hand signal that will mean stay—an open-handed gesture with the palm toward your dog's face. Take one step away, and at the same time, release the pressure on the leash.

If your dog moves or gets up, tell him "No!" so that he knows he made a mistake and put him back into position. Repeat the exercise. After a few seconds, go back to him and praise him. Don't let him move from his position until you release him. Use the same process to teach the stay in the down position.

With the stay command, you always want to go back to your Pit Bull to release him. Don't release him from a distance or call him to come from the stay. If you do either of these, your dog will be much less reliable on the stay—he will continue to get up from the stay because you will have taught him to do exactly that. When teaching the stay, you want your Pit Bull to learn that stay means "Hold this

position until I come back to you to release you."

As your Pit Bull learns the stay command, you can *gradually* increase the time you ask him to hold it. However, if your dog is making a lot of mistakes and moving often, you are either asking your dog to hold it too long or your dog doesn't understand the command yet. In either case, go back and reteach the exercise from the beginning.

Increase the distance you move away from your dog very gradually, too. Again, if your dog is making a lot of mistakes, you're moving away too quickly. Teach everything very gradually. When your Pit Bull understands the stay command but chooses not to do it, you need to let him know the command is not

Good dog! A well-trained Pit Bull knows that stay means he should hold this position until his owner says otherwise.

Photo by Isabelle Francais

american pit bull terrier

USING THE STAY COMMAND

You can use the stay command around the house. For example, in the evening while you're watching a favorite television show, have your Pit Bull lie down at your feet while you sit on the sofa. Give him a toy to chew on and tell him, "Sweetie, stay." Have him do a down/stay when your guests visit so he isn't jumping all over your guests. Have him lie down and stay while the family is eating so he isn't begging under the table. There are a lot of practical uses for the stay. Just look at your normal routine and see where this command can work for you.

when you're out in public and your dog is distracted by children playing or dogs barking behind a fence.

Start by having your Pit Bull sit in front of you. Have a treat in your right hand. Let him sniff the treat and then tell him, "Sweetie, watch me!" as you take the treat from his nose up to your chin. When his eyes follow the treat in your hand and he looks at your face, praise him, "Good boy to watch me!" and give him the treat. Then release him from the sit. Repeat it again exactly the same way two or three times and

The watch me exercise uses a treat or favorite toy to get and hold the dog's attention.

optional. Many young, wiggly Pit Bulls want to do anything except hold still. However, holding still is very important to Pit Bull owners. Correct excess movement first with your voice, "No! Be still! Stay!" and if that doesn't stop the excess movement, use a verbal correction and a snap and release of the leash. When he does control himself, praise him enthusiastically.

Watch Me

The watch me exercise teaches your Pit Bull to ignore distractions and pay attention to you. This is particularly useful

then quit until the next training session.

Because this is hard for young, bouncing Pit Bulls, practice it first at home when there are few distractions. Make sure your dog knows it well before you take him outside and try to practice it with distractions. However, once he knows it well inside, then you need to try it with distractions. Take him out in the front yard (on a leash, of course) and tell him to watch you. If he ignores you, take his chin in your left hand (with the treat in the right) and hold his chin so that he has to look at your face. Praise him even though you are helping him do it.

When he will watch you out front with some distractions, move on to the next step. Have him sit in front of you and tell him to watch you. As he watches you, take a few steps backward and ask him to follow you and watch you at the same time. Have him sit, and then praise him when he does. Try it again. When he can follow you six or seven steps and watch you at the same time, make it more challenging—back up and turn to the left or right, or back up faster. Praise him when he continues to watch you.

Heel

You want your Pit Bull to learn that "Heel" means "Walk by my left side with your neck and shoulders by my left leg, and maintain that position." Ideally, your Pit Bull should maintain that position as you walk slow, fast, turn corners, or weave in and out through a crowd.

To start, practice a "watch me" exercise to get your dog's attention on you. Back away from him and encourage him to follow and watch you. When he does, simply turn your body as you are backing up so that your dog ends up on your left side,

Do you walk your Pit Bull or does he walk you? Teach your dog to heel, and you can take back control of your exercise sessions.

Photo by Isabelle Francais

When he's first learning to heel, your Pit Bull will be easily distracted. Simply back away from him when this happens to keep his attention on you.

leash with a snap-and-release motion to make the dog follow you. Praise him when he does.

Don't hesitate to go back and forth—walking forward and then backing away; walking forward and backing away—if you need to do so. In fact, sometimes this can be the best exercise you can do to get your dog's attention on you.

When your dog is walking nicely with you and paying attention to you, then you can start eliminating the first step of backing away. Start the heel with your Pit Bull sitting by your left side. Tell him, "Sweetie, watch me! Heel." Start walking. When he's walking nicely with you, praise him. However, if he gets distracted or starts to pull, simply back away from him again.

and continue walking. If you have done it correctly, it is one smooth movement so you and your dog end up walking forward together with your dog on your left side.

Let's walk it through in slow motion. Sit your dog in front of you and do a "watch me." Back away from your dog and encourage him to follow you. When he's watching you, back up toward your left and as you are backing, continue turning in that direction so that you and your dog end up walking forward together. Your dog should end up on your left side and you should end up on your dog's right side.

If your dog starts to pull forward, simply back away from him and encourage him to follow you. If you need to do so, use the

USE IT OR LOSE IT

The best way to make this training work for you and your Pit Bull is to use it. Training is not just for training sessions, it is for your daily life. Incorporate it into your daily routine. Have your Pit Bull sit before you feed him. Have him lie down and stay while you eat. Have him sit and stay at the gate while you take the trash cans out. Have him do a down/stay when guests come over. Use these commands as part of your life. They will work much better that way.

All About
FORMAL
Training

Formal dog training is much more than the traditional sit, down, stay, and come commands. Dog training means teaching your Pit Bull that he's living in your house, not his. It means you can set some rules and expect him to follow them. It will not turn your Pit Bull into a robot, but instead it will teach your Pit Bull to look at you in a new light. Training will cause you to look at him differently, too. Training is not something you do *to* your Pit Bull; it's something you do together.

FINDING AN INSTRUCTOR OR TRAINER

When trying to find an instructor or trainer, word-of-mouth referrals are probably the best place to start. Although anyone can place an advertisement in the newspaper or yellow pages, the ad itself is no guarantee of quality or expertise. However, happy customers will demonstrate their experience with well-behaved dogs and will be glad to tell

Where did your neighbor's well-behaved dogs receive their training? Word-of-mouth referrals are the best way to find a good instructor.

Photo by Robert Pearcy

you where they received instruction.

Have you admired a neighbor's well-behaved dog? Ask where they went for training. Call your veterinarian, local pet store, or groomer, and ask who they recommend. Make notes about each referral. What did people like about this trainer? What did they dislike?

Once you have a list of referrals, start calling the instructors and ask a few questions. How long has she been teaching classes? You will want someone with experience, of course, so that she can handle the various situations that may arise. However, experience alone is not the only qualification. Some people that have been training for years are still teaching exactly the same way they did many years ago and have never learned anything new.

Ask the instructor about Pit Bulls. What does she think of the breed? Ideally, she should be knowledgeable about the breed, what makes them tick, and how to train them. If she doesn't like the breed—and some trainers don't like Pit Bulls—go elsewhere.

Ask the instructor to explain her training methods. Does this sound like something you would be comfortable with? Ask if there are alternative methods used. Not every dog will respond the same way, and every instructor should have a backup plan.

Does the instructor belong to any professional organizations? The National Association of Dog Obedience Instructors (NADOI) and the Association of Pet Dog Trainers (APDT) are two of the more prominent groups. Both of these organizations publish regular newsletters to share information, techniques, new developments, and more. Instructors belonging to organizations such as these are more likely to be up-to-date on training techniques, styles, and so forth, as well as information about specific dog breeds.

Make sure, too, that the instructor will be able to help you achieve your goals. For example, if you want to compete in obedience trials, that instructor should have experience in that field and knowledge of the rules and regulations concerning that competition.

After talking to several trainers or instructors, ask if you can watch their training sessions or classes. If they say no, then cross them off your

Photo by Robert Pearcy

Observing a class is one way to find out if you and your Pit Bull will be comfortable with a trainer's methods.

american pit bull terrier

list. There should be no reason why you cannot attend one class to see if you will be comfortable with this instructor and her style of teaching. As you watch the class, see how she handles students' dogs. Would you let her handle your dog? How does she relate to the students? Are they relaxed? Do they look like they're having a good time? Are they paying attention to her?

After talking to the instructor or trainer, and after watching a class, you should be able to decide which class you want to attend. If you're still undecided, call the instructor back and ask a few more questions. After all, you are hiring her to provide a service and you must be comfortable with your decision.

GROUP CLASSES OR PRIVATE LESSONS?

There are benefits and drawbacks to both group classes and private lessons. In group classes, the dog must learn to behave around other distractions, specifically the other dogs and people in class. Because the world is made up of lots of things capable of distracting your Pit Bull, this can work very well. In addition, a

Group classes are a great place for both you and your dog to make friends while you learn.

group class can work like group therapy for dog owners. The owners can share triumphs and mishaps and can encourage and support one another. Many friendships have begun in group training classes.

The drawback to group classes is that for some dogs the distractions of a group class are too much. Some dogs simply cannot concentrate at all, especially in the beginning of training. For these dogs, a few private lessons may help enough so that the dog can join a group class later. Dogs with severe behavior problems—especially aggression—should bypass group classes for obvious reasons.

Private lessons—one-on-one training with the owner, dog, and instructor—are also good for people with a very busy schedule who may otherwise not be able to do any training at all.

Training Methods

If you were to talk to 100 dog trainers (someone who trains dogs) or dog obedience instructors (someone who teaches the dog owner how to teach his dog) and ask them how they train, you would get 100 different answers. Any trainer or instructor who has

GOALS FOR YOUR PIT BULL

What do you want training to accomplish? Do you want your Pit Bull to be calm and well behaved around family members? Do you want him to behave himself out in public? Would you like to participate in dog activities and sports? There are an unlimited number of things you can do with your Pit Bull. It's up to you to decide what you would like to do. Then you can find a training program to help you achieve those goals. As you start training, talk to your trainer about them so she can guide you in the right direction.

been in the business for any period of time is going to work out a method or technique that works best for her. Each method will be based on the trainer's personality, teaching techniques, experience, and philosophy regarding dogs and dog training. Any given method may work wonderfully for one trainer but may fail terribly for another.

Because there are so many different techniques, styles, and methods, choosing a particular instructor may be difficult. It is important to understand some of the different methods so that you can make a reasonable decision.

Private lessons are a good idea if your Pit Bull can't concentrate in group settings or is aggressive toward other dogs.

Photo by Isabelle Francais

Compulsive Training

Compulsive training is a method of training that forces the dog to behave. This is usually a correction-based training style, sometimes with forceful corrections. This training is usually used with law enforcement and military dogs and can be quite effective with hard-driving, strong-willed dogs. Many pet dog owners do not like this style of training, feeling it is too rough.

Inducive Training

This training is exactly the opposite of compulsive training. Instead of being forced to do something, the dog is induced or motivated toward proper behavior. Depending on the instructor, there are few or no corrections used. This training works very well for puppies, dogs with mild personalities, and sometimes for owners who dislike corrections of any kind.

Unfortunately, this is not always the right technique for Pit Bulls. Many Pit Bulls will take advantage of the lack of corrections or discipline. Some very intelligent, very dominant-personality dogs (including some Pit Bulls) look upon the lack of discipline as weakness (on your part) and will then set their own rules—which, unfortunately, may not be the rules you wish them to abide by.

Somewhere in the Middle

The majority of trainers and instructors use a training method that is somewhere in between both of these techniques. An inducive method is used when possible, while corrections are used when needed. Obviously the range can be vast, with some trainers leaning toward more corrections and others using as few as possible.

Photo by Isabelle Francais

Compulsive training may be effective with particularly hard-driving, stubborn Pit Bulls, but it should never be attempted by an amateur.

TRAINING OPTIONS

Puppy Class

Puppy or "kindergarten" classes are for puppies over 10 weeks of age but not over 16 weeks. These classes are usually half obedience training and half socialization, because for puppies, both of these subjects are very important. The puppy's owner also learns how to prevent problem behaviors from occurring and how to establish household rules.

Whenever possible, Pit Bulls should attend puppy classes. The socialization, both with other puppies (of other breeds) and with other people, is very important for Pit Bulls.

Basic Obedience Class

This class is for puppies that have graduated from a puppy class, for puppies over four months of age that haven't attended a puppy class, or for adult dogs. In this class, the dogs and their owners work on basic obedience commands, such as sit, down, stay, come, and heel. Most instructors also spend time discussing problem prevention and problem solving, especially the common problems like jumping on people, barking, digging, and chewing.

Dog Sports Training

Some instructors offer training for one or more of the

various dog activities or sports. There are classes to prepare you for competition in obedience trials, conformation dog shows, flyball, agility, or schutzhund. Other trainers may offer training for noncompetitive activities, such as therapy dog work.

Advanced Training

Advanced training classes vary depending on the instructor. Some offer classes to teach you to control your dog off leash, some emphasize

dog sports, and others may simply continue basic training skills. Ask the instructor what she offers.

BUILDING A RELATIONSHIP

Training helps build a relationship between you and your dog. This relationship is built on mutual trust, affection, and respect. Training can help your dog become your best friend—a well-behaved companion that is a joy to spend time with and one that won't send your blood pressure sky-high!

Most trainers use a combination of compulsive and inducive training techniques, but every trainer's style and method is unique.

Photo by Isabelle Francais

american pit bull terrier

The relationship between you and your dog is built on mutual trust, affection, and respect—and it all begins with good training.

american pit bull terrier

Problem
PREVENTION
and Solving

Pit Bulls are an intelligent breed, but that's not the problem. Pit Bulls do, however, have an incredible stubborn streak that can get them into a lot of trouble. Because Pit Bulls are also easily trained, many Pit Bull owners are flabbergasted when they find that their dog has chewed up the wooden deck in the backyard or dismantled the picnic table.

Some Pit Bulls get themselves in hot water more often than their owners would like, although this guy seems to prefer it cold.

Photo by Isabelle Francais

TRAINING

Training can play a big part in controlling problem behavior. A fair, upbeat, yet firm training program teaches your dog that you are in charge and that he is below you in the family pack. The training should also reinforce his concept of you as a kind, calm, caring leader. In addition, your training skills give you the ability to teach your dog what is acceptable and what is not.

Unfortunately, problem behavior can have many causes, and solving it isn't always easy.

Many of the behaviors that dog owners consider problems—barking, digging, chewing, jumping up on people, and so on—aren't problems to your Pit Bull. In fact, they are very natural behaviors to your Pit Bull. Dogs dig because the dirt smells good or because there's a gopher in the yard. Dogs bark to verbalize something just as people talk. However, most problem behavior can be addressed and either prevented, controlled, or in some cases, stopped entirely.

WHAT YOU CAN DO

Exercise

Exercise is just as important for your Pit Bull as it is for you. Exercise works the body, uses up excess energy, relieves stress, and clears the mind. How much exercise is needed depends on your dog and your normal routine. A fast-paced walk might be enough for an older Pit Bull, but a young, healthy Pit Bull might need a good run or game of fetch with a tennis ball.

Photo by Isabelle Francais

Pit Bulls are athletic dogs that need plenty of exercise and playtime.

Play

Play is different from exercise, although exercise can be play. The key to play is laughter. Researchers know that laughter is wonderful medicine. When you laugh, you feel better about the world around you.

Laughter and play have a special place in your relationship with your Pit Bull. Pit Bulls can be very silly, and you should take advantage of that. Laugh at him and with him. Play games that will make you laugh. Play is also a great stress reliever—make time for play when you are having a hard time at work. Play with your Pit Bull after your training sessions.

Sometimes dogs get into trouble intentionally because they feel ignored. To these dogs, any attention—even corrections or yelling—is better than no attention at all. If you take time regularly to play with your dog, you can avoid some of these situations.

Health Problems

Some experts think that 20 percent of all common behavior problems are caused by health problems. A bladder infection or a gastrointestinal upset commonly causes housetraining accidents. Thyroid problems can cause a behavior change, as can medications, hyperactivity, hormone imbalances, and a variety of other health problems.

If your dog's behavior changes, make an appointment with your veterinarian. Tell your vet why you are bringing the dog in—don't just ask for an exam. Tell your vet that your Pit Bull has changed his behavior, tell him what the behavior is, and ask if he could do an exam for any physical problems that could lead to that type of behavior.

Don't automatically assume your dog is healthy. If a health problem is causing the behavior change, training or behavior modification won't make it better. Before beginning any training, talk to your veterinarian. Once health problems are ruled out, then you can start addressing the problem.

Nutrition
Nutrition can play a part in causing or solving behavior

Good nutrition can sometimes solve behavior problems. Foods containing high levels of linoleic acid will help to maintain a healthy skin and shiny coat in your dog; foods containing high levels of digestible proteins are also desirable. Photo courtesy of Nutro Products, Inc.

problems. If your dog is eating a poor-quality food, or if he cannot digest the food he is being fed, his body may be missing some vital nutrients. If your Pit Bull is chewing on rocks or wood, chewing the stucco off the side of your house, or grazing on the plants in your garden, he may have a nutritional deficiency of some kind.

Some dogs develop a type of hyperactivity when fed a high-calorie, high-fat dog food. Other dogs have food allergies that may show up as behavior problems. If you have any questions about the food your dog is eating, talk to your veterinarian.

Prevent Problems from Happening

Because so many of the things we consider problems are natural behaviors to your Pit Bull, you need to prevent as many of them from happening as you reasonably can. Put the trash cans away so that he never discovers that the kitchen trash can is full of good-tasting surprises. Make sure the kids put their toys away so that your Pit Bull can't chew them to pieces. It's much easier to prevent a problem from happening than it is to break a bad habit later.

Preventing a problem from happening might require that you fence off the garden, build higher shelves in the garage, or maybe even build your Pit Bull a dog run.

Part of preventing problems from occurring also requires that you limit your dog's freedom. A young puppy or untrained dog should never have unsupervised free run of the house—there is simply too much he can get into. Instead, keep him close to you and close off rooms. If you can't watch him, put him into his run or out in the back yard. A dog run is a safe place for your Pit Bull to relax or play outside while he is unsupervised.

A dog run is a safe place for your Pit Bull to relax or play outside while he is unsupervised.

Photo by Isabelle Francais

A DOG RUN

A dog run is not a dog prison; instead, it is a safe place for him where he can stay while he's unsupervised. In his dog run he should have protection from the sun and weather, unspillable water, and a few toys. Don't put him in his run as punishment, and never scold him in his run. Instead, give him a treat or a toy when you put him in his run. Leave a radio playing quiet, gentle music in a nearby window.

DEALING WITH SPECIFIC PROBLEMS

Jumping on People

You can control jumping up by emphasizing the sit. If your Pit Bull is sitting, he can't jump up. By teaching him to sit for petting, praise, treats, and for his meals, you can teach him that the sit is important and that everything he wants will happen only when he sits.

Use the leash as much as you can to teach your Pit Bull to sit. Because they are such solid, muscular dogs, Pit Bulls can be tough to hold onto unless you have something to grab hold of. The leash is your best training tool. When you come home from work, don't greet your dog

until you have a leash and collar in hand. As your dog greets you, slip the leash over his head. Then you can help him sit. If he tries to jump, give him a snap and release of the leash and a verbal correction, "No jump! Sit!" Of course, as with all of your training, praise him when he sits.

When you are out in public, make sure your Pit Bull sits before any of your neighbors or friends pet him. Again, use your leash. If he won't sit still, don't let anyone pet him even if you have to explain your actions, "I'm sorry, but I'm trying to teach him manners and he must sit before he gets any petting."

The key to correcting jumping up is to make sure the bad behavior is not rewarded. If someone pets your Pit Bull when he jumps up, that jumping up has been rewarded. However, when he learns that he only gets attention when he's sitting, that will make sitting more attractive to him.

Digging

If your backyard looks like a military artillery range, you need to concentrate first on *preventing* this problem from occurring. If you come home from work to find new holes in the lawn or garden, don't correct your dog then. He probably dug the holes when you first left in the morning, and a correction ten hours later won't work.

Instead, build him a dog run and leave him there during the day. If you fence off one side of your yard alongside your house, you might be able to give him a run that is 6 feet wide by 20 feet long. That's a great run. Let your dog trash this section to his heart's content—that's *his* yard.

Then, when you are home and can supervise him, you can let him have free run of the rest of *your* yard. When he starts to get into trouble, you can use your voice to interrupt him, "Hey! What are you doing? Get out of the garden!"

The destructive dog also needs exercise, training, and playtime every day to use up his energy and stimulate his mind so that he can spend time with you. Most importantly, don't let a dog that loves to dig watch you garden. If you do, he may come to you later with all of those bulbs you planted earlier.

The Barker

Pit Bulls are not normally problem barkers. However, a Pit Bull left alone for many hours

Photo by Isabelle Francais

Don't reward bad behavior, even if it's only on special occasions. You'll confuse your dog and make training more difficult.

each day may find that barking gets him attention, especially if your neighbors yell at him.

Start teaching him to be quiet when you're at home with him. When your Pit Bull starts barking, tell him, "Quiet!" When he stops, praise him. When he understands what you want, go for a short walk outside, leaving him home. Listen, and when you hear him start barking, come back and correct him. After a few corrections, when he seems to understand, ask a neighbor to help you. Go outside and ask your neighbor to come talk to you. Have the kids out in the yard playing. When your dog barks because he's feeling left out, go back and correct him. Repeat as often as you need to until he understands.

RUNNING FREE

If your Pit Bull does make it out through a door or gate, don't chase him. The more you chase, the better the game, as far as he's concerned. Instead, go get your shaker for training him to come. Shake it, "Sweetie, do you want a cookie? Come!" When he comes back to you, you must praise him for coming even though you may want to wring his neck for dashing through the door. Don't correct him. A correction will make him avoid you even more the next time it happens.

You can reduce your dog's emotional need to bark if you make coming home and leaving home quiet and low-keyed. When you leave the house, don't give him hugs or tell him repeatedly to be a good dog—that simply makes your leaving more emotional. Instead, give him attention an hour or two prior to your leaving. When it's time for you to go, just go.

When you come home, ignore your dog for a few minutes. Then whisper hello to him. Your Pit Bull's hearing is very good, but to hear your whispers he is going to have to be quiet and still.

You can also distract your dog when you leave. Take a brown paper lunch bag and put a couple of treats in it—maybe a dog biscuit, a piece of carrot, and a slice of apple. Roll the top over to close it and rip a very tiny hole in the side to give your dog encouragement to get the treats. As you walk out the door or gate, hand this to your dog. He will be so busy figuring out where the treats are and how to get them, he'll forget you are leaving.

Dashing Through Doors and Gates

This is actually one of the easier behavior problems to solve. Teach your Pit Bull to sit at all doors and gates, then hold that sit until you give him permission to go through or to get up after you have gone through. By teaching him to sit and wait for permission, you will eliminate the problem.

Start with your dog on leash. Walk him up to a door. Have him sit, tell him to stay, and then open the door in front of him. If he dashes through, use the leash to correct him (snap and release) as you give him a verbal correction, "No! Stay!" Take him back to his original position and do it again. When he will hold it at this door, go to another door or gate and repeat the training procedure.

When he will wait (while on leash) at all doors and gates, then take his leash off and hook up his long line. Fasten one end of the long line to a piece of heavy furniture. Walk him up to the door and tell him to sit and stay. Drop the long line to the ground. With your hands empty, open the door and stand aside. Because your hands are empty (meaning you aren't holding the leash) your Pit Bull may decide to dash. If he does, the long line will stop him or you can step on the line. Give him a verbal correction, too, "No! I said stay!" and bring him back to where he started. Repeat the training session here and at all other doors and gates.

OTHER PROBLEMS?

Many behavior problems can be solved or at least controlled using similar techniques. Try to figure out why your Pit Bull is doing what he's doing (from his point of view, not yours). What can you do to prevent the problem from happening? What can you do to teach your dog not to do it? Remember, as with all of your training, a correction alone will not change the behavior. You must also teach your dog what he *can* do.

If you still have some problems, or if your dog is showing aggressive tendencies, contact your local dog trainer or behaviorist for some help.

Teach your Pit Bull to sit at all doors and gates until you have given him permission to go through.

Advanced
TRAINING
and Dog Sports

Do you like training your Pit Bull? If you and your Pit Bull are having a good time, you may want to try one or more dog activities or sports. There are a lot of different things you can do with your dog—some are competitive, some are fun, some are good works—what you decide to do depends on you and your dog.

CONFORMATION COMPETITION

The United Kennel Club (UKC) awards conformation championships to purebred dogs registered with them. A championship is awarded when a purebred dog competes against other dogs of his breed several times (depending on the number of times competing and

Conformation competitions might be a good activity for you and your well-trained American Pit Bull Terrier.

Photo by Isabelle Francais

american pit bull terrier

Photo by Isabelle Francais

If you think your American Pit Bull Terrier is very handsome, attend a few dog shows to see how he compares to other dogs. If he matches the UKC standard, he may do well in conformation.

american pit bull terrier

the number of dogs, total) and wins. When competing, the judge compares each dog against a written standard for his breed and chooses the dog that most closely represents that standard of excellence.

This is a very simplistic explanation. However, if you feel your Pit Bull is very handsome, you might want to go watch a few local dog shows. Watch the Pit Bulls competing and talk to some of the Pit Bull owners and handlers. Does your Pit Bull still look like a good candidate? You will also want to do some reading about your breed and conformation competition and perhaps even attend a conformation class.

OBEDIENCE COMPETITION

Obedience competition is a team sport involving you and your Pit Bull. There are set exercises that must be performed in a certain way, and both you and your dog are judged on your ability to perform these exercises. The UKC sponsors obedience competitions for all breeds of dog, including Pit Bulls. There are also independent obedience competitions or tournaments held all over the country.

Before you begin training to compete, write to the sponsoring organization and get a copy of the rules and regulations pertaining to competitions. Go to a few local dog shows and watch the obedience competitions. See who wins and who doesn't. What did they do differently? There are also a number of books on the market specifically addressing obedience competition. You may want to find a trainer in your area who specializes in competition training.

AGILITY

Agility is a fast-paced sport in which the dog must complete a series of obstacles correctly in a certain period of time, with the fastest time winning. Obstacles might include tunnels, hurdles, an elevated dog walk, and more. The AKC, the UKC, and the United States Dog Agility Association all sponsor agility competitions. Although Pit Bulls are athletic dogs, they are not known for their extreme speed over a long course. Therefore, Pit Bulls do participate in agility for fun and training, but they are usually not competitive with faster breeds like Border

Collies and Shetland Sheepdogs.

FLYBALL

Flyball is a great sport for dogs that are crazy about tennis balls. Teams of four dogs and owners compete against each other. The dogs—one per team at a time—run down the course, jump four hurdles, and then trigger a mechanism that spits out a tennis ball. The dogs then catch the ball, turn, jump the four hurdles again, and return to their owner. The first team to complete the relay wins. Pit Bulls can run and jump with the best of athletic dogs but are usually not as fast as Border Collies, Australian Shepherds, or Shetland Sheepdogs and therefore aren't usually as competitive. In addition, some Pit Bulls get overstimulated by the team aspect of the sport— especially other dogs running and jumping. If your Pit Bull shows any signs of dog aggression whatsoever do *not* attempt to participate in this sport.

CANINE GOOD CITIZEN

The Canine Good Citizen (CGC) program was instituted by the American Kennel Club (AKC) in an effort to promote and reward responsible dog ownership. During a CGC test, the dog and owner must complete a series of ten exercises, including sitting for petting and grooming, walking nicely on the leash, sit, down, stay, and come. Upon the successful completion of all ten exercises, the dog is awarded the title "CGC." For more information about CGC tests,

You and your athletic Pit Bull might enjoy training for and competing in agility trials. This Pit Bull and his owner are learning a new obstacle.

contact a dog trainer or dog training club in your area. The CGC is open to all dogs, including Pit Bulls, even though Pit Bulls are not registered with the AKC.

TEMPERAMENT TEST

The American Temperament Test Society was founded to provide breeders and trainers with a means of uniformly evaluating a dog's temperament. By using standardized tests, each dog would be tested in the same manner. The tests can be used to evaluate potential or future breeding stock, future working dogs, or simply as a way for dog owners to see how their dog

might react in any given situation.

For information about temperament tests in your area, contact a local trainer or dog training club.

THERAPY DOGS

Dog owners have known for years that our dogs are good for us, but now researchers are agreeing that dogs are good medicine. Therapy dogs go to nursing homes, hospitals, and children's centers to provide warmth, affection, and love to the people who need it most. Pit Bulls make great therapy dogs. Contact your local dog trainer or animal shelter for information about a group in your area.

Pit Bulls have a lot of love to share. They often make great therapy dogs, visiting people in nursing homes, hospitals, and other facilities.

SCHUTZHUND

Schutzhund is a sport that originated in Germany to evaluate working dogs. Dogs are trained and tested in obedience, tracking, and protection work. Protection work must be undertaken with a great deal of forethought, because teaching a dog to bite is serious and a potential liability. However, when undertaken with *good training* and *responsibility*, schutzhund is a reputable, legitimate sport for Pit Bulls.

HAND SIGNALS

When you start teaching hand signals, use a treat in your hand to get your Pit Bull's attention. Use the verbal command he already knows to help him understand what you are trying to tell him. As he responds, decrease the verbal command to a whisper and emphasize the hand signal.

The difficult part of teaching hand signals is that in the beginning, your dog may not understand that these movements of your hand (and arm) have any significance. After all, people "talk" with their hands all the time—hands are always moving and waving. Dogs learn early to ignore hand and arm movements. Therefore,

WEIGHT OR WAGON PULLING

As mentioned earlier in this book, Pit Bulls have been said to be the strongest breed of dog in the world for their size. This makes weight-pulling competitions perfect for Pit Bulls, and in fact, Pit Bulls have dominated many weight-pulling competitions.

In this sport, dogs are harnessed to a sled or wagon loaded with a measured weight (usually piles of bags of dog food). The dogs must pull the sled or wagon down a straight, measured course and are timed while pulling. Your dog trainer might be able to guide you toward a local competition and give you some pointers as to how to prepare your dog for weight pulling.

If you have no desire to compete in weight-pulling competitions, you can still use your dog's strength. Teach him to pull a wagon. When you have 40 pounds of dog food to bring in, let him pull it up to the house in his wagon. He can drag the trash cans out to the curb. Harness that strength! My sister's Pit Bull, Dillon, pulls the baby and kids in the wagon when they go out for a walk. He also pulls the groceries home from the store. Talk to your dog trainer for information about adapting a kid's wagon to the dog and how to train the dog to safely pull a wagon.

to make hand signals work, your Pit Bull needs to watch you. A good treat in the hand making the movement can help.

In order to learn a hand signal, your dog must watch you carefully.

Down

When you taught your Pit Bull to lie down by taking a treat from his nose to the ground in front of his front paws, you were teaching him a hand signal. Granted, he was watching the treat in your hand, but he was also getting used to seeing your hand move. Therefore, switching

USING HAND SIGNALS

Dog owners often think of hand signals as something that only really advanced dogs can respond to, and that is partly right. It does take some training. However, hand signals are useful for all dog owners. For example, if your dog responds to hand signals, you can give him the signal to go lie down while you're talking on the telephone, and you won't have to interrupt your conversation to do so.

him over from verbal command to a hand-signal-only command should be easy.

Have your dog sit in front of you. Verbally, tell him "Down" as you give him the hand signal for down (with a treat in your hand), just as you did when you were originally teaching it. When he lies down, praise him and then release him. Practice it a few times.

Now give him the signal to go down (with a treat in your hand) but do not give a verbal command. If he lies down, praise him, give him the treat, and release him. If he does not go down, give the leash a slight snap and release down toward the ground—not hard—but just enough to let him know, "Hey! Pay attention!" When he goes down, praise and release him.

When he can reliably follow the signal with no verbal command, make it more challenging. Signal him to lie down when you are across the room from him, while you're talking to someone, and when there are some distractions around him. Remember to praise him enthusiastically when he goes down on the signal.

Sit

If you were able to teach your Pit Bull to sit using the treat above his nose, you were teaching him to sit using a hand signal. If you had to teach him by shaping him into a sit, you can still teach him a signal.

With your Pit Bull on the leash, hold the leash in your left hand. Have a treat in your right hand. Stand in front of your Pit Bull and take the treat from his nose upward. At the same time, whisper "Sit." When he sits, praise him and release him. Try it again. When he is watching your hand and sitting reliably, stop whispering the command and let him follow the signal. If he doesn't sit, jiggle the leash and collar to remind him that something is expected. Again, when he sits, praise him.

The hand signal for the come command begins with an outstretched arm, then sweeps wide toward the chest.

american pit bull terrier

Stay

When you taught the stay command, you used a hand signal, the open-palmed gesture toward your Pit Bull's face. This signal is so obvious your dog will probably do it without any additional training. Have your dog sit or lie down and tell him to stay using only the hand signal. Did he hold it? If he did, go back to him and praise him. If he didn't, use the leash to correct him (snap and release) and try it again.

Come

You want the signal for the come command to be a very broad, easily seen signal; one that your dog can recognize even if he's distracted by something. Therefore, this signal will be a wide swing of the right arm, starting with your arm held straight out to your side from the shoulder, horizontal to the ground. The motion will be to bring the hand to your chest following a wide wave, as if you were reaching out to get your dog and bring him to you.

Start teaching the signal by having the shaker you used to teach the come command in your right hand as you start the signal. Shake it slightly—just to get your dog's attention—and

then complete the signal. Praise your dog when he responds and comes to you.

If he doesn't respond right away, start the signal again and this time tell him (verbally) to come as you are making the signal (and shaking the shaker). Again, praise him when he comes. Gradually eliminate the verbal command, and when your Pit Bull is responding well, gradually stop using the shaker.

Pit Bulls are notorious for pulling their owners along on the leash. They are great candidates for a no-pull training halter that's guaranteed to stop any dog of any size or weight from ever pulling again, without choking the dog. Photo courtesy of Four Paws.

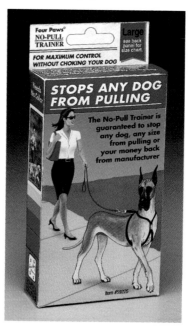

OFF-LEASH CONTROL

One of the biggest mistakes many dog owners make is to take the dog off the leash too soon. When you take your dog off the leash, you have very little control; only your previous training can control your dog. If you take your dog off leash before you have established enough control, or before your dog is mentally mature enough to accept that control, you are setting yourself up for disaster.

Pit Bulls are smart, curious dogs, and they love to check out new things, especially new smells. A rabbit is made to chase as far as Pit Bulls are concerned, and so is a butterfly or bird. More than one Pit Bull has been so involved in his exploring that he's forgotten to pay attention to his owner's commands.

BE CAUTIOUS

If your Pit Bull has shown any signs of aggression at all to people or other dogs, *never* take him off leash outside of a fenced-in, secure area where you can control access. To assume that your dog is safe *most* of the time is asking for a disaster to happen. Be safe—protect your dog, other people, and other dogs.

Before your Pit Bull is to be allowed off leash (outside of a fenced yard or your backyard), you need to make sure your Pit Bull's training is sound, which means he should be responding reliably and well to all of the basic commands.

Your Pit Bull must also be mentally mature, and in some Pit Bulls that might be two, two-and-a-half, or even three years of age. He should be past the challenging teenage stage of development. Never take an adolescent off leash outside of a fenced-in area—that is setting the young dog up for a problem.

Come on a Long Line

The long line (or leash) was introduced earlier in the section on teaching the come command. It is also a good training technique for preparing your dog for off-leash control. Review that section and practice the come on a long line until you are comfortable that your dog understands the come command from 20 to 30 feet away (the length of the long line) and will do it reliably.

Now take him out to play in a different place that is still safe and free from dangers—a schoolyard is good. Let your Pit Bull drag his long line behind him as you let him sniff and

Photo by Isabelle Francais

Never let a young dog off leash in public. Wait until he is grown up, well trained, and mentally mature.

explore. When he's distracted and not paying attention to you, call him to come. If he responds right away, praise him enthusiastically. Tell him what a smart, wonderful dog he is!

If he doesn't respond right away, step on the end of the long line, pick it up, and back away from your dog, calling him again as you use the long line to make him come to you. Don't beg him to come to you or repeat the come command over and over. Simply use the line to make him do it. This is not an optional command!

Heel

Most places require that dogs in public be leashed. However, teaching your Pit Bull to heel without a leash is a

good exercise. Not only is it a part of obedience competition (for people interested in that sport), but it's a good practical command, too. What would happen if your dog's leash or collar broke when you were out for a walk? Accidents happen, and if your dog has already been trained to heel off leash, disaster would be averted.

To train for this, hook two leashes up to your dog's collar. Use your regular leash and then a lightweight leash. Do a watch me with treats and then tell your dog to heel. Practice a variety of things—walk slow, fast, turn corners, and perform figure eights. When your dog is paying attention well, reach down and unhook his regular leash, tossing it to the ground in front of him. If he bounces up, assuming he's free, correct him with the second leash, "Hey! I didn't release you!" and make him sit in the heel position. Hook his regular leash back up and repeat the exercise.

When he doesn't take advantage of the regular leash being taken off, then tell him to heel and start practicing the heel. Do not use the second leash for minor correction but save it for control. If he tries to dash away, pull from you, or otherwise break the heel exercise, use that second leash and then hook his regular leash back on again.

Repeat this, going back and forth between one leash and two, until he's not even thinking about whether his regular leash is on or not. You want him to work reliably without questioning the leash's control. For some Pit

Bulls, this may take several weeks worth of work.

When he is working reliably, put the second leash away. Take his regular leash, hook it up to his collar and fold it up. Tuck it under his collar between his shoulder blades so that it is lying on his back. Practice his heel work. If he makes a mistake, grab the leash and collar as a handle and correct him. When the correction is over, take your hand off.

Expect (and demand) the same level of obedience off leash that you do on leash. Don't make excuses for off-leash work.

OFF-LEASH SAFETY

When training any off-leash command, do it safely. Think of any possibilities and how you might handle them *before* they happen!

Knowing that your off-leash Pit Bull will respond to your commands will allow you to relax and enjoy your playtime together.

Photo by Isabelle Francais

american pit bull terrier

Have Some
FUN
With Your Training

Training your Pit Bull can be serious, and in many cases, it has to be serious business. After all, a Pit Bull with no manners (or poor manners) can be a dangerous dog. However, training can also be fun. Games and trick training can challenge your training skills and your Pit Bull's ability to learn. Once you have taught your dog, though, you can have a great time showing off your dog's tricks, amusing your friends, and just plain having fun with your dog.

Trick training is fun, especially when you have a Pit Bull that loves to show off.

Photo by Isabelle Francais

RETRIEVING

Some Pit Bulls like to retrieve—they just don't always understand the need to bring back what they go out after. However, once you teach your Pit Bull to bring back the toy, retrieving games can be great fun as well as good exercise.

If your Pit Bull likes to retrieve, then all you need to

GREAT EXERCISE
Pit Bulls need daily exercise, and a walk around town is not to be considered adequate exercise! However, a daily game of retrieve can be good exercise. Throw the ball or Frisbee™ for 30 to 45 minutes, and you can use up some of your dog's excess energy.

do is get him to bring you back the toy. When you throw the toy and he goes after it, wait until he picks it up. Once he has it in his mouth, call him back to you with a happy tone of voice. If he drops the toy, send him back to it. If he brings the toy all the way back to you, praise him enthusiastically.

Teaching your Pit Bull the names of his toys is a great way to make him think.

Don't let him play tug-of-war with the toy. If he grabs it and doesn't want to let go, reach over the top of his muzzle and tell him "Give," as you press his top lips against his teeth. You don't have to use much pressure, just enough so that he opens his mouth to relieve the pressure. When he gives you the toy, praise him.

If your Pit Bull likes to take the toy and run with it, let him drag his long line behind him while he plays. Then, when he dashes off, you can step on the line and stop him. Once you've stopped him, call him back to you.

THE NAME GAME

The name game is a great way to make the dog think. And don't doubt for a minute that your Pit Bull can think! When you teach your Pit Bull the names of a variety of things around the house, you can then put him to work, too. Tell him to pick up your keys, your purse, or send him after the remote control to the television. The ideas are unlimited.

Photo by Isabelle Francais

What tricks do you want your dog to learn? Use your imagination to think of unique, fun ways to teach your dog to display his talents.

CAUTION!

Do not teach a *puppy* to pick up anything other than his toys. You can teach him the names of different toys, but do not teach him to pick up the television remote, your keys, or anything else of yours until he is grown up and mentally mature. Otherwise, your things will end up all chewed to pieces!

Start with two items that are very different, perhaps a tennis ball and a magazine. Sit on the floor with your Pit Bull and place the two items in front of you. Ask him, "Where's the ball?" and bounce the ball so that he tries to grab it or at least pays attention to it. When he touches it, praise him and give him a treat.

When he is responding to the ball, lay it on the floor and send him after it. Praise and reward him. Now set several different items out with the magazine and ball and send him after the ball again. When he is doing well, start all over again with one of his toys. When he will get his toy, then put the toy and ball out there together and send him after one or the other. Don't correct him if he makes a mistake, just take the toy away from him and try it again. Remember, he's learning a foreign language (yours) at the same time he's trying to figure out what the game is, so be patient.

FIND IT!

When the dog can identify a few items by name, you can then start hiding those items so that he can search for them. For example, once he knows the word "keys," you can drop your keys on the floor under an end table next to the sofa. Tell your Pit Bull, "Find my keys!" and help him look. Say "Where are they?" and move him toward the end table. When he finds them, praise him enthusiastically.

THE COME GAME FOR PUPPIES

Two family members can sit on the ground (or floor) across the yard or down the hallway from each other. Each should have some treats for the puppy. One family member calls the puppy across the yard (or down the hall), and when the puppy reaches her, she should praise the puppy and give him a treat. She then turns the puppy around so that he's facing the other family member, who calls the puppy. This very simple game can make teaching the come command exciting for the puppy. In addition, kids can play this game with the puppy, giving them a chance to participate in the puppy's training.

As he gets better, make the game more challenging. Make him search in more than one room. Have the item hiding in plain sight or underneath something else. Help him in the beginning and when he appears

HAVE FUN WITH TRICKS

I taught one of my dogs to play dead, and we both had a lot of fun with it. Michi got so good he could pick the phrase "dead dog" out of casual conversation. One day, the son of a neighbor of mine had just graduated from the police academy and was very proud of his new uniform. Michi and I were out front, so we went over to congratulate the new police officer. As I shook the police officer's hand, I turned to Michi and asked him, "Would you rather be a cop or a dead dog?" Michi dropped to the ground, went flat on his side, and closed his eyes. The only thing giving him away—that he really was having fun—was the wagging tail! Meanwhile, my neighbor's son was stuttering and turning red. He didn't know whether to be offended or to laugh. It was great fun!

confused—but don't let him give up. Make sure he succeeds.

HIDE AND SEEK

Start by having a family member pet your Pit Bull, offer him a treat, and then go to another room. Tell your Pit Bull, "Find Dad!" and let him go. If he runs right to Dad, praise him! Have different family members play the game, and teach the dog a name for each of them so that he can search for each family member by name.

As he gets better at the game, the family member hiding will no longer have to pet the dog at the beginning of the game, he can simply go hide. Help your dog initially so that he can succeed at the game but encourage him, too, to use his nose and his scenting abilities.

SHAKE HANDS

Shaking hands is a very easy trick to teach. Have your dog sit in front of you. Reach behind one front paw, and as you say, "Shake!" tickle his leg in the hollow just behind his paw. When he lifts his paw, shake it gently and praise him. When he starts lifting his paw on his own, stop tickling.

WAVE

When your dog is shaking hands reliably, tell him "Shake. Wave!" and instead of shaking his paw, reach toward it without taking it. Let him touch his paw to your hand, but pull your hand away so that he's waving. Praise him. Eventually, you want him to lift his paw higher than for the shake and to move it up and down so he

Learning to shake hands is easy for most dogs and makes a great first trick.

american pit bull terrier

Photo by Isabelle Francais

The roll-over is a popular trick. With practice, you can even teach your Pit Bull to do multiple rolls.

looks like he's waving. You can do that with the movements of your hand as he reaches for it. Praise him enthusiastically when he does it right. When he understands the wave, you can stop your hand movements.

ROLL OVER

With your Pit Bull lying down, take a treat and make a circle with your hand around his nose as you tell him, "Roll over." Use the treat (in the circular motion) to lead his head in the direction you want him to roll. Your other hand

may have to help him. Pit Bulls have a big rib cage, and it may take some effort on your dog's part to start the roll-over movement.

MAKE UP YOUR OWN TRICKS

What would you and your Pit Bull have fun doing? Teach him to stand up on his back legs and dance. Teach him to jump through a hula hoop or your arms forming a circle. Teach him to play dead or to sneeze. Trick training is limited only by your imagination and your ability to teach your dog.

SUGGESTED READING

BOOKS BY T.F.H. PUBLICATIONS

JG 113
*The New Owner's Guide to
American Pit Bull Terriers*
Todd Fenstermacher
160 pages, 150 full-color photos

JG 117
*The New Owner's Guide to Dog
Training*
Dorman Pantfoeder
160 pages, over 100 full-color photos

JG-109
Training The Perfect Puppy
Andrew DePrisco
160 pages, over 200 color photos

TS 283
Training Problem Dogs
Dr. Louis Vine
256 pages, 50 drawings